Air Superiority

Above:

Blowpipe in southern Belize, where it could be called upon to demonstrate its effectiveness against surface targets. Shorts is developing variants for armoured vehicles and helicopters, and the advanced microcomputer Javelin system is now also in production. *MoD*

Air Superiority

BILL GUNSTON

IA

LONDON

IAN ALLAN LTD

United States distribution by

Motorbooks International
Publishers & Wholesalers Inc
Osceola, Wisconsin 54020, USA   ®

First published 1985

ISBN 0 7110 1417 5

Published by Ian Allan Ltd, Shepperton, Surrey;
and printed by Ian Allan Printing Ltd at their works
at Coombelands in Runnymede, England.

Above:
**One of the flightlines at the TWCU (Tornado
Weapons Conversion Unit) at Honington. A purely
national RAF unit, TWCU dropped its 15,000th bomb
as this book was being written.** *BAe*

Previous page:
**Two Bitburg Eagles on patrol carrying no external
stores apart from the 600 US gal centreline tank. The
later F-15C not only has improved radar and
software but also carries conformal (FAST) fuel
pallets along the sides, while the F-15E will carry a
24,000lb weapon load in the attack role. Both will
probably eventually be based in Europe.**
USAFE

Contents

Preface

This book is an overview of the actual confrontation between the air forces of the Warsaw Pact nations and those of the NATO countries in the final quarter of the 20th century. It pays particular attention to the situation in Europe, which is almost universally regarded as the place where the battle would take place should the Politburo in the Kremlin – which has absolute power over the forces of all Warsaw Pact countries – decide there was a chance of winning a military campaign against NATO.

In general this book complements Ian Allan's 'Modern Combat Aircraft' series, which deals primarily with the hardware. Instead, though inevitably some discussion of the hardware is necessary, this volume is concerned with force structures, investment, policy decisions (or lack of them), and particularly with how the opposing forces in the European theatre stack up against each other. It attempts to add flesh to the dry bones of statistics by talking about such intangibles as individual personnel capability and morale, the possible effect of the introduction of new technology by either side, and by no means least public opinion.

Whenever two groups of humans confront each other, inevitably they will have sharply differing views of the situation. Probably each will think it has right on its side. Perhaps each will think it is weak and innocent, whilst confronted by a vastly stronger and belligerent opponent. Each will believe its own members are fortunate not to have to live in the repressive police state on the other side. In such circumstances it is not easy to try to present the truth.

This book does attempt to do this, but when one is confronted by a totalitarian regime it is difficult to retain one's original concept of the meaning of truth. Many readers will notice with a chill down the spine that this book was written in the year that was the title of a best-selling novel by George Orwell published almost 30 years earlier. The fictitious country portrayed therein – which at the time seemed scarcely credible – had propaganda mottoes that 'black is white, white is black, truth is fiction and fiction is truth'. To suggest that such rules apply daily to the Soviet propaganda machine is hardly news to anyone who studies the historical record. This is surely tragic, but the Soviet Union has from its very birth been geared to the projection of Communism and the erosion of Capitalism, using words as much as bullets or threats, and it is almost certainly no longer capable of even approaching the reporting of facts or events with a 'naive' open mind.

When one is dealing with megatons the truth becomes rather important, not only for the media copywriter but for most of the life on our planet.

There is no simple way to try to convey a 'truthful' picture of a military balance of power. The most basic way of all might be to draw a map of the relevant regions and then draw in every aircraft, every armoured vehicle, every soldier, and so forth. But at once there would be arguments over what should be included: aircraft type A is obsolete, even though hundreds are still in front-line service, aircraft B should not be included because it is only just entering service, aircraft C should not be included because it is an advanced trainer (even though it carries powerful weapons), and so on. During the SALT discussions the Soviets suggested that, in return for NATO not deploying either cruise missiles or Pershing 2, a number of SS-20 launchers would be withdrawn and moved back beyond the Urals. In other words, for NATO having none of these modern deterrent weapons, a vastly more powerful and much longer-ranged Soviet weapon would be resited in places where every missile, each with three thermonuclear warheads, could still cover the whole of Western Europe. Big deal!

The overall situation in the mid-1980s is so horrifying that it needs no exaggeration. Some of the most frightening areas of all, such as thermonuclear strategic forces and the mobile land armies, are outside the coverage of this book. In fact the air is the only area in which there is a semblance of parity between NATO and the WP forces, there being a broad similarity in aircraft quality and aircrew proficiency, and a ratio in

numbers (excluding Soviet aircraft outside the European theatre) officially put at 2,975 NATO against 7,240 WP. This ratio is far better than in such areas as main battle tanks, where it is virtually no-contest! Unfortunately, the already slightly worrying imbalance in combat aircraft is backed up by ratios far exceeding 3:1 against NATO in such matters as SAMs and Triple-A (anti-aircraft artillery).

In the crucial matter of electronic warfare numerical data is hard to come by, but the official consensus is that WP air forces are much better and more uniformly equipped than those of NATO with Elint, ESM and active ECM to help each aircraft to fly each mission with a good chance of success and a safe return to base. How can it be that the RAF, world leader in airborne EW systems in 1944, should 40 years later have no active jammers in NATO front-line service other than a few picked up cheap secondhand from the USAF? The answer is obvious: lack of money. What a nation can accomplish in war is governed by many things, but money ranks high on the list.

Sadly, while the Politburo simply takes decisions based on what is needed (the common people being neither informed nor asked for their opinion), in Western countries free debate has led to the growth of several movements dedicated to eroding the ability of Western countries to defend themselves. The massive nuclear protest movement professes to be against all nuclear weapons in all countries; but, as it cannot exist except in the West, where freedom of speech is maintained by those same weapons, it is only the West's defences that are under siege. An even more inverted and nonsensical protest movement is popularly called the Neo-Luddites. The Luddites were organised mobs who early in the 19th century dedicated themselves to the destruction of spinning, weaving and knitting machines throughout Britain, and they had later supporters who tried to prevent the introduction of steam power, iron-hulled steamships, steam railways and almost every other new invention. The Neo-Luddites are dedicated to campaigning against high technology, and very especially high-technology weapons. Thanks in part to curiously motivated stories in the media, the US public has to a remarkable degree come to believe that the so-called 'military-industrial establishment' has for years wasted public money on a prodigious scale with unwanted and ineffective armaments packed

with costly electronics and many other items which the common herd do not understand.

Nobody in the media has any incentive to inform the public or even help defend the Free World against the colossal and growing threat posed by the Soviet Union. The task of the media is to sell papers or get more viewers, and this is best done by creating controversial 'stories'. Waste in defence has been a sure-fire winning angle for the past 20 years, so today we have the situation in which we in the West not only cannot afford to defend ourselves but we have positive antipathy to (a) weapons that deter war, and (b) weapons that offer greater capability whilst cutting down on uniformed manpower.

Is it not paradoxical that in the Free World, guarded by armed forces so few in number that they are never seen by the public except at ceremonial parades, the media should regard these forces as either of no news value or as targets for (often misinformed) attack, while in the Soviet Union the public can hardly open a newspaper without seeing pictures captioned 'our heroes' or 'on guard'? This book cannot do much about the propaganda angle, but at least it can try to outline how the NATO and WP air forces stack up against each other. It is impossible to attempt this without expressing opinions, many of which will be highly controversial. Not least, the real proof of any pudding is in the eating, and the author hopes as fervently as everyone else in the Western world that the information on how these air forces would actually perform in warfare will forever be denied to us.

Bill Gunston
Haslemere, Surrey
1984

The Threat

Historically, the VVS (*Voyenno-Vozdushnye Sili*, or air force) of the Soviet Union has been biassed almost totally to support of the land army in a land battle. One must not ignore such other projections of aerospace power as the PVO (aerospace defence of the homeland), VTA (war transport aviation) and AVMF (air forces of the navy), and at the strategic and political level the king of all Soviet forces is the mighty RVSN (strategic rocket forces). This book, however, is concerned mainly with tactical air forces, and this branch, until recently called the FA (*Frontovaya Aviatsiya*, or Frontal Aviation) in the Soviet Union, has since its formation immediately after World War 2 been the central core of the VVS.

This concentration upon tactical airpower is a natural result of the Soviet Union's enormous frontier which abuts many hostile nations. Until the mid-1930s Soviet tactical airpower was constantly engaged in active warfare against dissidents within the Soviet Union itself. Stalin himself admitted that 10 million *kulaks* (land-owning farmers) had been 'liquidated' for resisting collectivization of their farms, while a special type of attack aircraft was developed to wipe out the *bazmashi* horsemen of Turkestan. Such activity, combined with large-scale and highly realistic exercises, led to the Soviet VVS being organised above all as a force for the support of ground forces fighting a land battle. It also resulted in a large and effective spectrum of tactical air weapons, including the world's best air machine guns and cannon, and unequalled expertise in the armouring of aircraft against hostile fire.

But Nazi Germany happened to attack the Soviet Union on 22 June 1941 at a time when the VVS was singularly ill-prepared, and losses in the first few weeks were staggering. Ever since, the Great Patriotic War has exerted a very important influence in Soviet affairs, serving on the one hand as proof of the wish of the capitalist world to destroy the Soviet state and on the other as a major reason for defence budgets which are gigantic by any standard, and which exert an enormous adverse effect upon all other branches of the Soviet economy. Had there been no Great Patriotic War it would have been more difficult to persuade the populations of all 15 republics of the Soviet Union that they must suffer a poor standard of living in order to support the greatest war machine the world has ever seen.

Incidentally, the supposed enmity of the capitalist nations is bolstered by suppressing the fact that they were allies of the Soviet Union in 1941-45. A quite senior Russian officer told the author how surprised he was when this fact emerged during his cadet training. The author can also vouch for the rewriting of history by the WP satellite countries. One of his daughters invited a teenage girlfriend from Budapest to stay, and she noticed a book on the Luftwaffe. 'How can you write about such a disgusting thing?' she asked. The author apologised, but mildly pointed out that Hungarian squadrons had flown on the same side. Furious, she said 'You are lying, you must have been

Right:
Ever since the Alliance was formed in 1949 the recurrent nightmare of NATO has been the spectre of massed Soviet hordes moving west, like a tidal wave breaking across Western Europe. *Novosti*

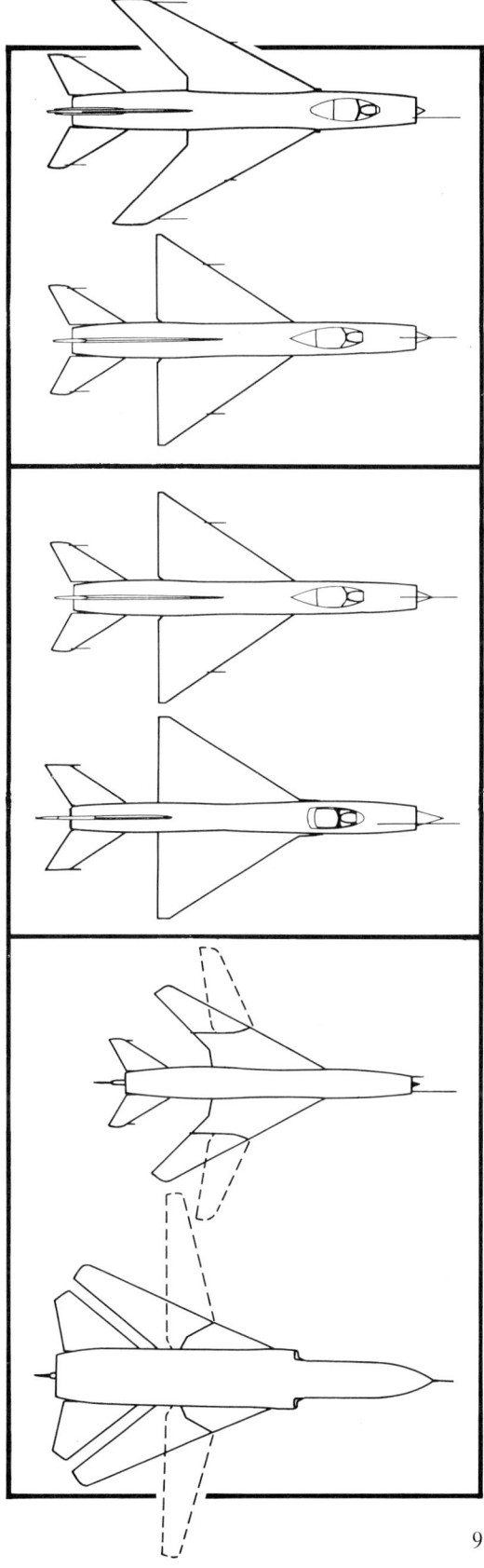

Right:
TsAGI, the Soviet national aerodynamics research centre, came up in 1955 with two 'best shapes' for the future crop of Mach 2 fighters, one with a 57° delta and the other a 60° slender swept wing. Both had tailplanes. The shapes are here seen on the Su-7B (which became a ground attack aircraft) and Su-11.

Centre right:
Having adopted a 'best shape', this was then used by different designers, often at different scales. Here an Su-11 and MiG-21 are seen to the same scale.

Bottom right:
In the 1960s TsAGI refined two forms of variable-geometry 'swing wing', one for modification of existing aircraft and the other for uninhibited new designs. The former, with pivots far apart, was used on the Su-22 (shown here) and Tu-22M; the other on the Su-24 (shown here) and MiG-23/27.

brainwashed!' There was no point in pursuing the matter.

In the immediate postwar era the Soviet Union had a lot of catching up to do, notably in jet propulsion, strategic bombers, radar and nuclear weapons. (Had the capitalist West really wished to defeat the Soviet Union, this was when it would have struck, when the atom bomb was its alone.) Thanks to effective spying, plus the gratuitous export from Britain of the West's best turbojet, the deficiencies were made good in short order. Where tactical airpower was concerned a significant discovery was the fact that the MiG-15 interceptor, when flown in the ground-attack role, could do essentially the same job as special-purpose *shturmovik* (armoured attack) aircraft, so for 25 years from 1953 the latter species disappeared from the FA inventory.

In 1955 the Soviet aerodynamic research centre, TsAGI, came up with two idealised shapes for supersonic combat aircraft, both with conventional tails but one with a delta wing and the other with an acutely (62°) swept wing. These shapes were used for many prototypes by the rival MiG and Sukhoi design bureaux, and while the delta was selected for the MiG-21, which has been built for 25 years in many versions, and for the bigger and totally specialised Su-9 and Su-11 interceptors (from which today's Su-15 was derived), the swept-wing shape was picked for the Su-7 attack aircraft. These types, the MiG-21 and Su-7 series, formed the backbone of Frontal Aviation throughout the 1960s and most of the 1970s.

The advent of the pivoted 'swing wing' was a matter of great concern to the Soviet designers. They had not invented it, and anything that puts Soviet aircraft at a disadvantage must be overcome with extreme urgency. The result was two new shapes, one an idealised one based pragmatically on the American F-111, but avoiding most of that aircraft's fundamental shortcomings, and the other an interim modification of existing aircraft with pivots far outboard to give improved performance with minimal risk and the shortest timescale. The interim solution was applied – with success far exceeding prediction – to the Su attack series, giving them a remarkable new lease of life, and on a much larger scale of size to the Tu-22 supersonic bomber/reconnaissance aircraft, rather unexpectedly frightening the Americans into thinking that the resulting Tu-22M ('Backfire') was almost in the class of the B-1 and aimed at the North American continent.

Despite the importance of the supposed interim swing-wing aircraft, which will remain in service for many years to come, it is the uncompromised swing-wing tactical attack aircraft that have come to dominate the Soviet Union's striking power against the NATO nations in Europe. Two types alone, the MiG-23/27 ('Flogger') and the Su-24 ('Fencer') easily outnumber all the tactical warplanes of all NATO countries based in Europe. Thanks to a sustained effort the WP air forces overtook the NATO European air forces in terms of numbers more than 20 years ago, but throughout the period 1958-78 no very deep knowledge of aircraft was needed to conclude that, on published performance figures, the NATO aircraft tended to have higher capability.

This NATO edge in unit or platform capability also extended to certain other types of weapon, including main battle tanks, battlefield communications and, in the early part of the time-frame, SAMs. Thanks to a further sustained effort by the Soviet Union, this qualitative superiority of important Western arms has been eroded, and in many cases turned into a qualitative deficiency (though this needs the qualification that it has often been gained without attention to such things as crew comfort or workload). Nowhere is the reversal of the former Western superiority more marked than in combat aircraft.

This is despite the introduction of substantial numbers of the F-16 aircraft, and smaller quantities of other replacements for older Western types, which have improved individual aircraft mission capability by an officially estimated 64% between 1965 and 1980. Over the same time period the Soviet and WP theatre aviation regiments increased the mission capability of their aircraft by an estimated 70%, and by 1983 the figure had been revised upwards to 77%. It is fair to point out that the WP forces were starting from a lower level, and so greater improvements were to be expected, but the fact that has to be recognised is that the emphasis in Soviet production of combat aircraft in the past 20 years has been very strongly on aircraft able to penetrate defended airspace over great distances and drop very effective loads of conventional or nuclear weapons.

As recently as 1978 the bulk of FA attack regiments were equipped with the MiG-21 and Su-7BM. Since that time there has been little change in numbers, but these older aircraft have been progressively replaced on a one-for-one basis by the MiG-23BN, MiG-27, Su-17M and Su-24. These show a marked increase in general level of sophistication, indicating a correspondingly higher capability among all support personnel. The preceding generation carried little electronic equipment beyond communications radio, a simple range-only radar and a basic passive warning receiver. (Even that was better than many contemporary NATO front-line aircraft.) All the newer types have an overall avionic and countermeasures fit superior to almost all NATO aircraft. They also gain in having large and robust engines more powerful than those fitted to any of the tactical fighter and attack aircraft of NATO.

A particularly potent threat is presented by the Su-24 ('Fencer'), because of its size, power and

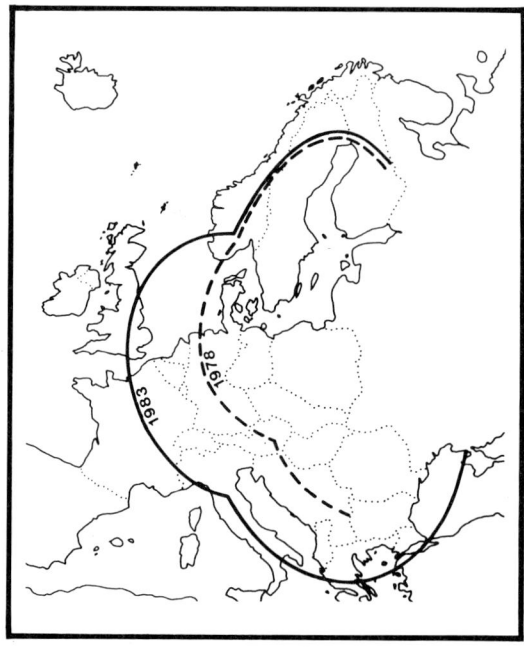

Right:
Thanks to the introduction of large numbers of the large and powerful Su-24 ('Fencer') the Soviet Frontal Aviation has greatly extended its attack radius, with approximately doubled bombloads. These curves show the mission radius in 1978 and 1983 on the demanding Lo-Lo-Hi profile; flying a Hi-Lo-Hi mission the Su-24 takes in the whole of Britain and France.

radius with a heavy offensive load. Its bomb load for any radius is much greater than that of the Lancaster, and even on a hi-lo-hi profile (ie, flying at the lowest safe height throughout the dangerous part of the mission, to avoid radar detection, until after the attack has been made) can take a bomb load of 17,637lb (8 tonnes) to targets in East Anglia or along the entire length of Italy. On a hi-lo-hi profile with reduced load it can attack targets anywhere in Great Britain, France or Spain.

Combined with this awesome attack radius has come vastly better navigational accuracy and reliability, a totally different order of delivery accuracy for free-fall weapons, and a wide and growing spectrum of precision attack missiles. One of the puzzles of the air-warfare scene has been the absence of tactical ASMs (air-to-surface missiles) from Soviet Frontal Aviation. Such weapons were used in large numbers by Hitler's Luftwaffe, and the American Bullpup and French AS.11 were well advanced in testing by 1956. Yet, though extremely large cruise missiles appeared under Soviet bombers by 1961, no tactical weapon was seen in the West until 1982. Admittedly, by that time several types were known to exist, and one of the problems was deciding which missile it was that appeared in a photograph of an Su-17 released in early 1982. The seemingly obvious guess was that it was the weapon known to NATO as AS-7 'Kerry', because this was numerically and chronologically the first of the FA's crop of ASMs, but in fact this guess was incorrect. AS-7 is larger, and the canard missile seen on the Su-17 is now thought to have been AS-10.

That these missiles are actually long established in VVS service is underscored by the remark of a Soviet air force general as far back as 1977. He said, 'If we can see our target, we can attack it. If we attack it, we can hit it. And with modern

weapons we certainly would expect to destroy it with the first shot.' Of course, it could be suggested that this is precisely the kind of remark that would be made by a senior officer of an air force that had completely failed to equip itself with modern precision attack weapons, yet still wished to intimidate its enemies. It is significant that, though such a counter-suggestion would very likely have been made 25 years ago, nobody was misguided enough to make it in 1977. Though we have already had something to say about Soviet manipulation of 'truth', when it comes to claims of weapon capability there is no example known to the author of such a Soviet claim being found to be false. We disbelieve such statements at our peril.

Of course, it goes without saying that today's VVS, and the WP air forces of the satellite nations, have moved very far from being a clear-visibility daylight force. With the MiG-21F and Su-7B the all-weather capability was almost zero, being roughly the same as for an F-86F or Hunter. By the late 1960s Soviet equivalents of VOR, DME and Tacan were used on all tactical aircraft, and an ILS was also almost universal. Today every attack aircraft has several items which are by no means found on all NATO tactical machines, including a radar altimeter, either a twin-gyro platform and doppler or a complete INS, a laser ranger and designator/marked-target seeker and, except in a very few cases, a multimode forward-looking radar and terrain-avoidance radar. The Su-24 has a complete TFR, said by Soviet pilots (who ought to be in a position to know) to be broadly similar to that fitted to IDS Tornado and markedly better than the TFR in the F-111E.

To a first-order approximation the MiG-27 can be regarded as comparable with the Jaguar, though it has getting on for double the engine thrust. Similarly the Su-24 can be regarded as an updated F-111 with all-round capability very close to that of IDS Tornado, though it is again far more powerful than either of the Western types. There is plenty of evidence, going back several decades, that the Soviet Union is intensely interested in weapons and military capability, and not particularly concerned at consumption of money, raw materials and fuel

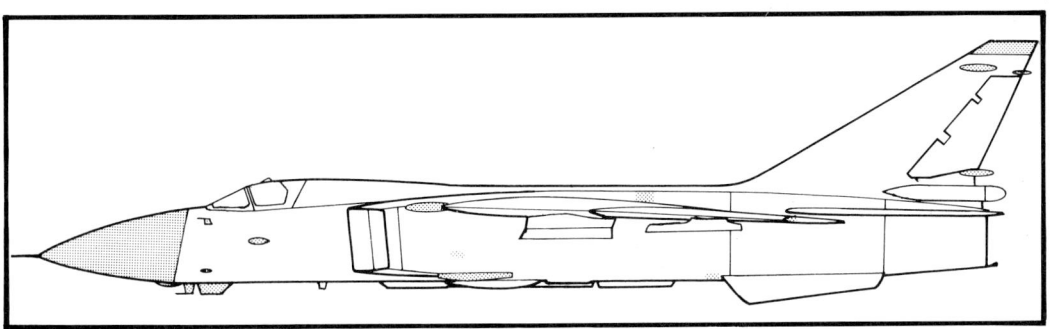

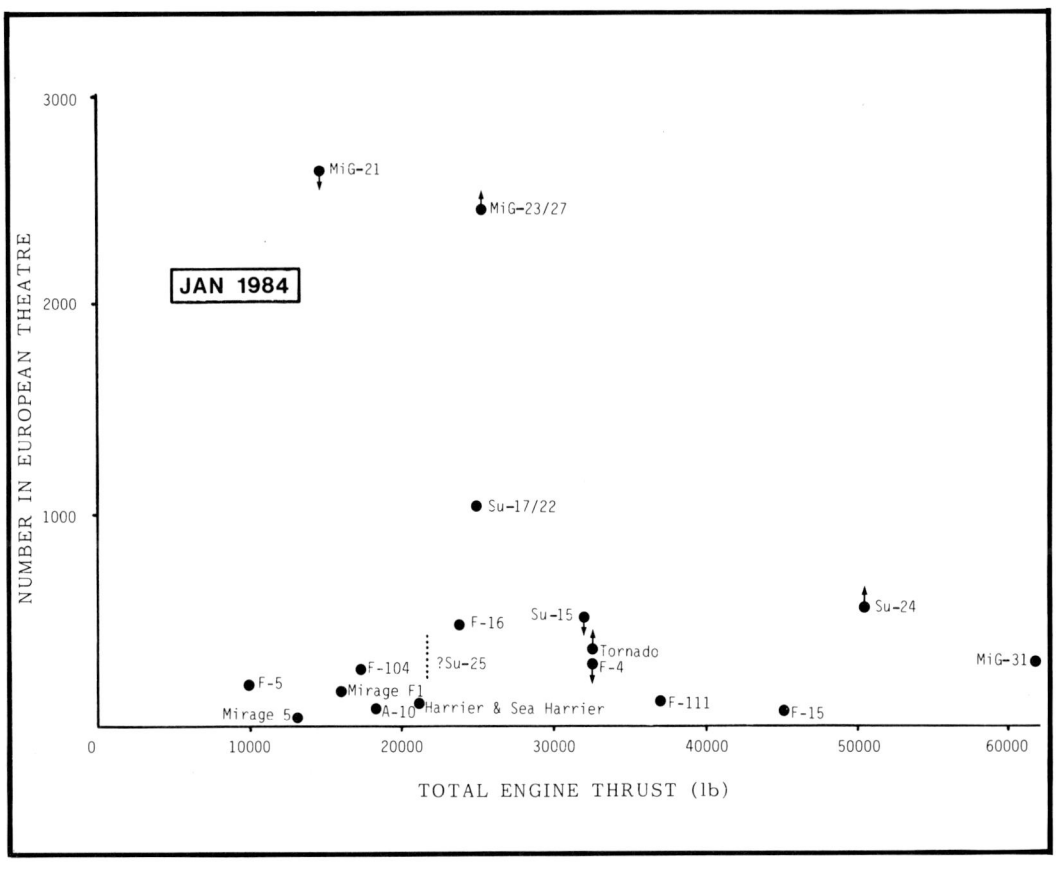

Above:
A fair first-order approximation of 'amount of airpower' (assuming constant levels of technology) is to multiply numbers of front-line aircraft by their engine thrust. This plot gives an idea of how things stood in the European theatre in January 1984.

(unless an item is strategically in short supply). One supposes that basic laws of arithmetic apply to the Soviet Union as to other countries, but the author has yet to hear of a single example of a proven and useful weapon whose procurement was denied or curtailed on grounds of its cost.

This is especially significant when one considers the almost mind-boggling investment made by the Soviets in the past 25 years building up armoured divisions, a deep-water offensive navy (including the world's largest force of ballistic-missile submarines) and a force of strategic thermonuclear ICBMs of utterly awesome power which alone consumed over 40% of the total defence budget in 1965-80. Such weapons are not considered here, but it is highly relevant to note that, far from any cutback, the Soviet Union is in 1984 well advanced with the world's biggest and most powerful

bomber, two completely new landbased ICBMs each far bigger than the USAF's proposed MX Peacekeeper, a new generation of cruise missiles for launch from land, sea and air, a new generation of SLBMs in parallel with submarines far bigger than any previously imagined, and expansion on a colossal scale of intermediate nuclear forces. None of this has any parallel in the West, because it cannot be afforded.

Though the emphasis in 1965-80 was on increasing the range, bombload, penetrative capability and all-weather delivery accuracy of attack aircraft, the VVS has since that time shown evidence of two further prongs of effort. One is the Su-25 ('Frogfoot'), a specialised close-support machine obviously inspired by the A-10. The other is a new generation of air-combat fighters. It has been known since World War 1 that, more than any other category of war weapon, the fighter aircraft has to be superior to its opposite numbers if it is to win. Admittedly this belief can sometimes be overturned by the brilliance of the pilot, but as a general rule the fighter wins by its own technical superiority. The fighter designer can never relax, and he has to get his parameters right. Things that matter are SEP (specific excess power), agility as measured by instantaneous and sustained rates of turn, the quality of the radar and cockpit displays, and the air-to-air weapons. Maximum speed is almost never of any interest.

The Soviet Union has always set a high standard in most of these variables, though some aircraft – most versions of MiG-21 are a prime example – have suffered from such shortcomings as short range or endurance, or inadequate weapons, or the need for a long airstrip. Outstanding Western aircraft, notably the F-15, kept the pressure on the Soviets and forced the development of a new fighter generation in the 1970s. These aircraft were further influenced in 1974 by the YF-16 and YF-17, and the final result is two new fighters, the MiG-29 and Su-27, quite apart from which the MiG bureau has also developed the extremely fast MiG-25 ('Foxbat') interceptor into the MiG-31. All three aircraft are formidable, as explained in Chapters 3 and 5.

It is interesting to note that, while the Soviet Union publicly professes to regard NATO as the only possible aggressor, its entire land and air armadas are tailored to a mobile war moving west. Even the large surveillance radars are designed for being uprooted and redeployed elsewhere, unlike the air-defence stations of NATO's NADGE chain which are irrevocably fixed. A further point which seems important to the author is that the best way to shoot down hostile aircraft overhead is to fire SAMs at them. The result with a good SAM system is likely to be a trading on the basis of one SAM for one hostile aircraft. The kill is quick and sure, in the sharpest contrast to the highly ineffective results of early SAM systems such as SA-7 and Redeye, and there is little risk to any friendly hardware or personnel. To fill the same airspace with friendly fighters causes an immediate identification problem, and to take a coldly practical view is likely to result in a trade on the basis of one of theirs for one of ours.

The Soviets have an absolute need for plentiful

and good air combat fighters, because if they are to take the war to NATO, moving westwards, the only SAMs on the ground ahead of the WP ground forces will belong to NATO. Fighters are the only way to gain command of the NATO airspace. Such air superiority is still important, even though the treetop penetrator travelling on TFR at 800kt can still streak through to its target without bothering about such matters. In any prolonged land campaign the side whose aircraft can occupy the sky with impunity has a colossal advantage. Such air supremacy is hardly likely ever to be achieved by NATO in the region occupied by WP land forces, because the dense phalanx of mobile radars and mobile SAMs/AAA would make it impossible; but NATO could still command its own airspace if the Soviets neglected to equip their regiments with the very best fighters, and in large numbers.

Of course, the notion that these Soviet fighters might have to go into battle against the NATO air forces' complete orbat (order of battle) is arrant nonsense. Soviet planners just do not do things the hard way, though they are certainly not squeamish about taking losses. The first thing that the NATO air forces would know about any impending war would be when they discovered that nobody was answering the telephone at the airbases, for the excellent reason that a 20-kiloton warhead had just detonated above each. The Soviet tactical and intermediate rocket forces can deliver so many warheads that it has proved a real problem finding targets for them, and most would be held in reserve. In the author's opinion – but not, it must be stressed, the official opinion of NATO, which professes to believe that the Soviet high command would never be so unsporting as to carry out a sneak nuclear strike – only the barest handful of NATO aircraft would ever get into the air on Day 1, and they would do so only because when the pre-emptive blow fell they happened to be somewhere else. Thus, the scenario to be encountered by the WP pilots is one of virtually empty skies, except for their own aircraft. Picking off any NATO survivors ought not to be particularly difficult.

Even if the Kremlin were to send a letter to SACEUR saying, 'With the greatest regret, war starts at 03.00 next Tuesday', there is very little that

Left:
Called SA-7 'Grail' by NATO, the first-generation Soviet infantry SAM (surface-to-air missile) has been made in astronomic numbers and used all over the world. The official NATO height limit continues to be 4,920ft (1,500m), though a Hunter over Oman was hit at 11,500ft (3,500m). Simple support frames like this one are common on Warsaw Pact Jeep-type vehicles. *MoD via Mike Gething*

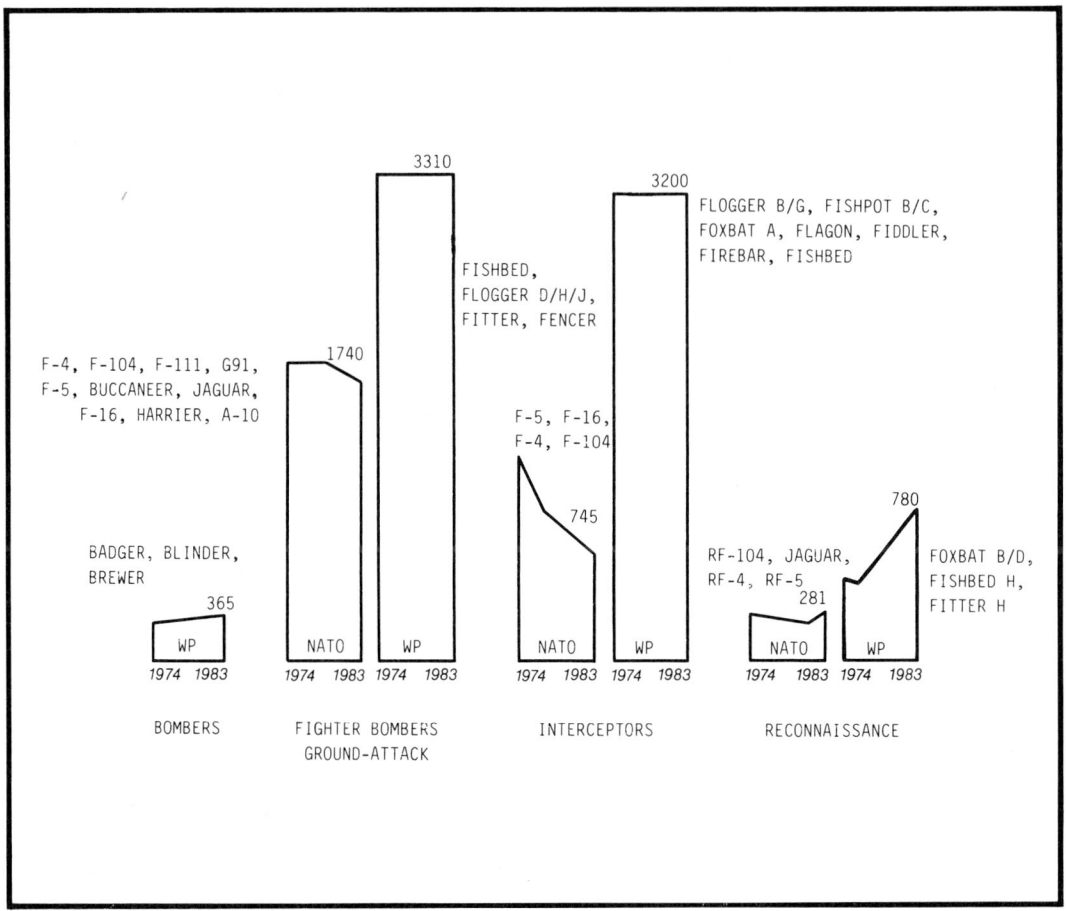

3310

3200

FLOGGER B/G, FISHPOT B/C,
FOXBAT A, FLAGON, FIDDLER,
FIREBAR, FISHBED

FISHBED,
FLOGGER D/H/J,
FITTER, FENCER

F-4, F-104, F-111, G91,
F-5, BUCCANEER, JAGUAR,
F-16, HARRIER, A-10

1740

F-5, F-16,
F-4, F-104

BADGER, BLINDER,
BREWER

745

780

RF-104, JAGUAR,
RF-4, RF-5

FOXBAT B/D,
FISHBED H,
FITTER H

365

281

WP	NATO	WP	NATO	WP	NATO	WP
1974 1983	1974 1983	1974 1983	1974 1983	1974 1983	1974 1983	1974 1983

BOMBERS   FIGHTER BOMBERS   INTERCEPTORS   RECONNAISSANCE
                     GROUND-ATTACK

Above:
**Broad comparison of numbers of aircraft in NATO
and WP air forces (excluding Moscow air-defence
district) in Europe, showing variation in each
category over the years 1974-1983. Many of the
interceptors can be used for ground attack. The
numbers refer to aircraft on the strength of combat
units.**

NATO could do about it. There is no great network
of secondary or reserve airbases. Even if there were
some places where the NATO air forces could
temporarily hide, they could neither operate from
those places nor return to their own fireballed
airfields. For all practical purposes, 100 SS-20s,
with three MIRV warheads apiece, could take care
of NATO airpower at the start of Day 1. Probably
the number actually assigned to this task is fewer
than 100.

One cannot help but be deeply impressed at the
apparent ability of the Soviet Union to leave no
stone unturned, to plan constantly for the best
weapons and the best-organised war machine, and
to find money for everything. In sharp contrast to
the narrow nationalist outlook of each of the 14 (or

is it up to 16 ?) NATO nations, the WP forces are
totally centrally controlled. They have virtually
100% interoperability of equipment, and in most
cases the equipment is standardised. Thus they
enjoy all the economies of scale which, for
shortsighted nationalist reasons, are denied to the
so-called Free World nations.

These advantages are accentuated by the
disparity in numbers between all kinds of war
weapons deployed by the two sides. As already
noted this contrast is least apparent in the matter of
combat aircraft, but even here it is in the order of
2½ to 1. And it is no longer possible to seek cosy
solace in a supposed technical inferiority of the
Soviet hardware. There have been many occasions,
for example with Russian aircraft in 1941 and
Japanese aircraft in 1942, when ignorance on the
part of the Western world automatically gave rise to
a supposition – presented as a sure belief – that the
unknown capability was far inferior to that of the
West. Gradually, as knowledge has replaced
ignorance, such beliefs have been shattered.

At the same time, it is almost equally easy to
replace scorn by exaggerated awe. Soviet

Right:
Though designed in 1954-59, the radio-guided SAM known to NATO as SA-3 'Goa' continues in widespread service in many forms. This 1974 photograph shows the only non-mobile form (in Egypt). Missile weight is 1,402lb (636kg). *SIPA*

capabilities are quite formidable and impressive enough without needing any elaboration or overstatement. A good guiding principle was enunciated by a member of the Carter Administration: 'The Russians aren't ten feet tall – but they're a good six foot, and growing.'

So far we have given an overview of the build-up of Soviet offensive air capability facing Europe, without going into detail on numbers or deployment. An accompanying set of bar charts (histograms) shows the relative numerical strengths of WP and NATO air forces broken down into four fixed-wing categories of aircraft. These comparisons include all NATO aircraft in Western Europe but exclude American aircraft in other theatres (including the USA) or at sea aboard carriers, British aircraft in the Falklands, French aircraft, and the aircraft of non-NATO countries. On the WP side the numbers are for aircraft actively facing NATO, and exclude all strategic and naval air forces, the Moscow Air Defence District and all forces elsewhere in the Soviet Union.

The figures, and especially the trends, are obviously disquieting to anyone in the Western world – not only Europeans. The charts are those first published in the standard 'NATO and the Warsaw Pact, Force Comparisons', updated to 1984. The figures for attack aircraft and interceptors have been modified by transferring approximately 1,100 units from the latter to the former category to reflect their actual employment (because they have stores pylons fitted, their pilots are qualified for attack missions and air/ground stores are held by the operating regiments).

To attempt to deploy its gigantic forces even more effectively the Soviet Supreme High Command (VGK) has since 1980 totally reshaped

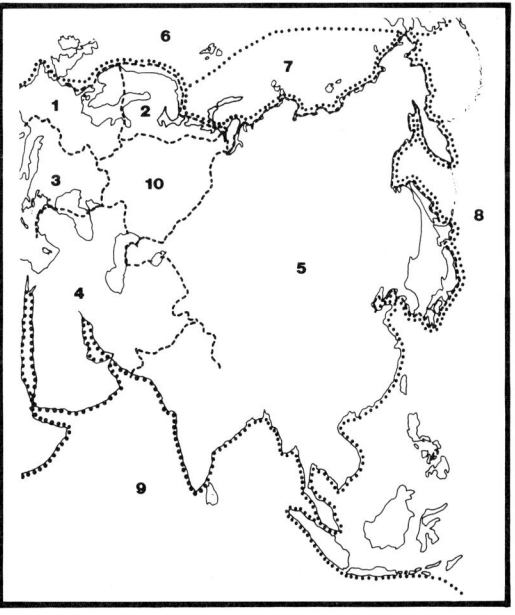

Right:
The entire Soviet military might is organised into TVDs (theatres of military operations). This map is based on that prepared by the US Department of Defense in 1983; numbers have altered little in 1984.

1 — **Central European TVD;** *2* — **Northern TVD;** *3* — **Southwest European TVD;** *4* — **Southern TVD;** *5* — **Far Eastern TVD;** *6* — **Atlantic OTVD;** *7* — **Arctic OTVD;** *8* — **Pacific OTVD;** *9* — **Indian Ocean OTVD;** *10* — **Central strategic reserve.**

Note: **Boundaries, particularly outside the USSR, remain speculative.**

its entire global command system. At the highest level it has spent enormous sums to ensure the survival of the national system of total state control by the CPSU (Communist Party of the Soviet Union). In the 1981 review of Soviet military power the US Department of Defense commented that 'Alternative locations have been established for virtually the entire structure of the Soviet leadership – political, military, security and industrial . . . many of these are bunkered facilities, and certain levels of leadership are provided with mobile equipment as well'. Quick-reaction, nuclear-hardened aircraft with very special communications are even now standing by 24 hours a day ready to take to the sky with the complete State Defence Committee (GKO), which includes not only the General Secretary of the CPSU, Konstantin Chernyenko and his successor in the job of head of the KGB, but also two of the key men in the Soviet Union, the Minister of Defence, D. F. Ustinov, and the First Deputy Minister and Chief of the General Staff, who until September 1984 was N. V. Ogarkov.

It was Ogarkov who, writing in *Kommunist* in July 1981, first publicly spelt out the rationale behind the massive reorganisation: 'It is not the front, but the larger form of military operations – the strategic operation in the theatre of military operations – which should be regarded as the basic operation in a possible future war.' Previously there was no geographically arranged global command structure, but just a subdivision of the Soviet Union, and the satellites and occupied territories in Europe, into 20 Military Districts (see map). These remain for the time being, but it is felt that they are much too localised for any future war, especially a nuclear one. So the world has been carved up into 13 TVDs (theatres of military operations, or more strictly 'theatres of war operations'), each covering a vast geographical area. The eight largest are by far the biggest areas ever put under a single military command, four being maritime TVDs and four intercontinental TVDs which include the Americas and other major land-masses. The other five cover the Soviet Union and the rest of Asia and Western Europe.

It is the last five TVDs that concern us here. They are called: Central Europe, Southwest Europe, South, Far East and North. Each TVD now has a unified command for all arms: thus the continental TVDs control five armies, or army groups; five FA air forces; and five PVO aerospace defence forces. Previously the FA was controlled on a mere frontal level, while the PVO was controlled at national level. There has been considerable transfer of equipment and personnel between the different branches. Though many of the aircraft are multirole, large numbers of fighters have been passed from the FA to the new TVD-based PVO

Top:
Seen here in the firing position for ceremonial purposes, the SA-9 'Gaskin' system uses a neat canard missile with a height limit of about 16,400ft (5,000m). Each BRDM-2 type scout car carries four launchers plus four reloads. SA-13 is an enlarged version, carried on the MT-LB amphibious tracked vehicle. *Tass*

Above:
Photographed here in a snowstorm, the SA-8 'Gecko' SAM system is carried, together with its complete multiple-aerial radar group and reload missiles, on a specially designed amphibious vehicle. Since 1980 the SA-8B version has been in use, with the four exposed ready-use missiles replaced by six in box containters. *Tass*

organisation, which has also taken over all the vast AAA/SAM forces previously part of the army. Thus, it is hoped that within each TVD the command structure will be totally flexible and totally integrated. Previously, for example, a hostile aircraft being tracked by the PVO might, in theory, fly right over an army SAM belt which had not been informed.

Of particular importance to this book are the substantial forces not committed to TVD command. One is the vast and terrifying RVSN, the strategic rocket forces. Another is the ICBM/SLBM warning system, the anti-ballistic missile defence network (which exists in the Soviet Union alone) and the growing anti-space forces. In addition we now have the newly formed AASU (Aviation Armies of the Soviet Union), which control the most powerful long-range striking forces with interdictors, bombers and cruise missiles. This has taken over not only the bombers previously administered by the DA (long-range aviation) but also the large and growing interdictor force equipped with the Su-24 ('Fencer'). These pose the greatest threat to Western Europe, other than the SS-11 and SS-20 nuclear missiles which have approximately 1,800 warheads targeted on NATO airfields, ports and cities in Europe. This reorganisation is expected to confer several big advantages. It is certainly almost ideally flexible, provides a common C^3 (command, control and communications) structure for all arms, and in the case of air striking power makes very strong forces available for use against any kind of target, at any distance.

At present there are three AASUs. Of these, three replace the DA, and operate large bombers: the 30th AASU has its HQ at Irkutsk (see map) and is equipped with Tu-22Ms, Tu-16s and Su-24s, and is expected to be the first to receive the new 'Blackjack' intercontinental bomber; the 36th AASU has its HQ in Moscow and is equipped with Tu-16s and M-4s and also will receive 'Blackjack'; and the 46th AASU has its HQ in Russia, at Smolyensk, in easy reach of European targets with its Tu-22s, Tu-22Ms and Tu-16s. There is doubt about whether any of the armies use any Tu-95s ('Bear') in the bomber role. Each of the three ex-DA air armies is believed to be made up of 12 regiments, and the total combat-ready strength exceeds 800 bombers. As Tu-22Ms are delivered they are usually replacing Tu-16s, which increasingly are serving in Elint and ECM reconnaissance and strike support roles.

Under the former FA the strength of Su-24s facing Western Europe built up to approximately 400 by spring 1982. According to several authorities there were pairs of regiments each with about 50 aircraft, based at Tukums, Latvia; Chyernyakhovsk, near Kaliningrad (former Königsberg); Starokonstantinov, Ukraine; and

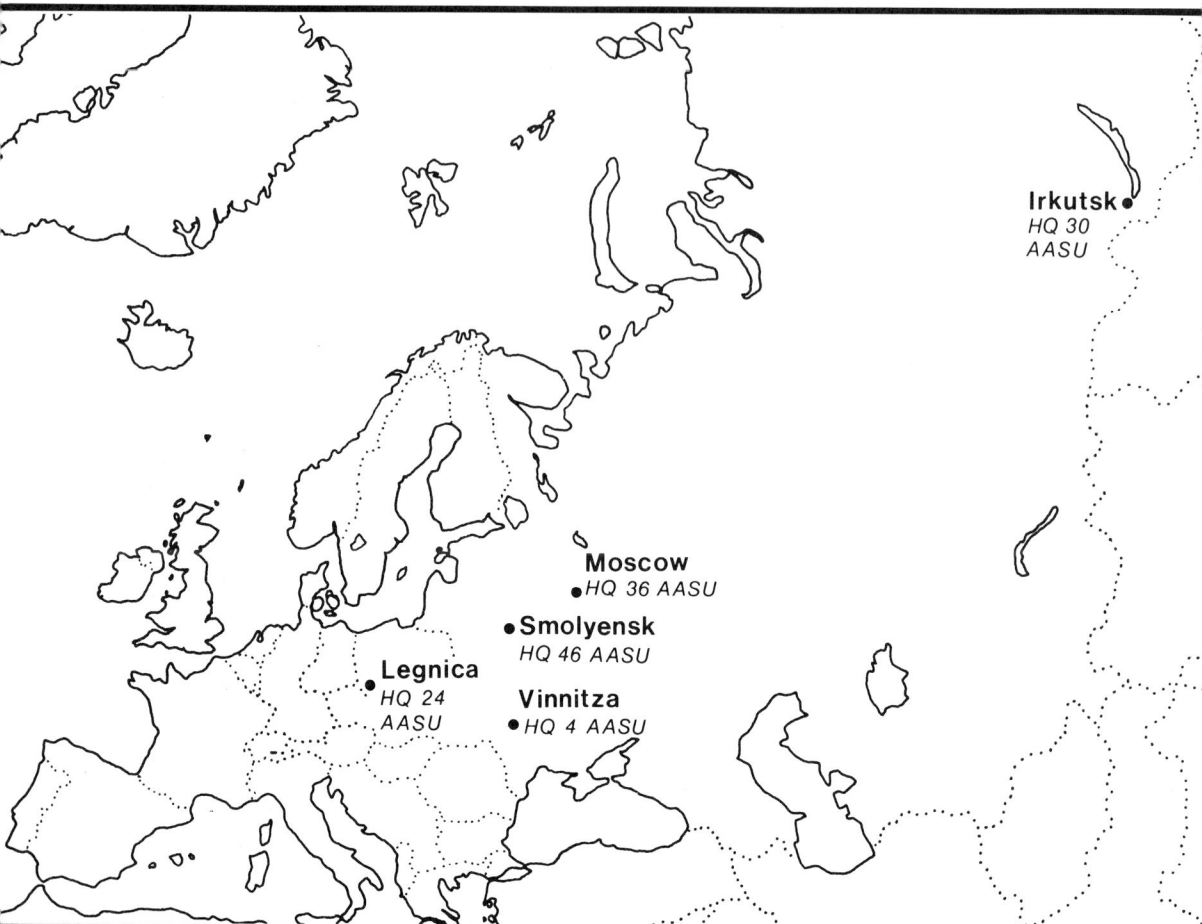

Above:
A simplified map showing national boundaries only, with locations marked of five of the giant Air Armies of the Soviet Union formed in 1983.

Gorodok, Ukraine. Today the main western Su-24 force numbers about 500, split into two AASUs, each with five regiments: the 24th (previously the 37th tactical air army), at Legnica, Poland; and the 4th, with HQ at Vinnitsa, Ukraine. It should be emphasised that all regiments of these Su-24 AASUs are regularly dispersed to off-airfield operation, as are almost all Soviet tactical aircraft, though this is not possible at maximum weight. Moreover, the five regiments of each AASU are at all times geographically dispersed among different airfields. There is evidence that considerable efforts continue to be made to provide austere operating platforms, with a prefab runway but hardly any above-ground buildings and little in the way of lighting or electronic aids (these might be highly

mobile) to increase dispersal capability in time of war. Such bases would be rolled up and moved with the advancing armies, and this is actually practised in WP exercises.

One area not so far touched upon is the Group of Soviet Forces in Germany (GSFG), which previously was the largest single component of the FA, styled the 16th Air Army. Most of the FA's tactical air armies were quite small, but the 16th had roughly 1,500 aircraft. In the event of war the Central Europe TVD would control all air forces in the DDR (East Germany), Poland and Czechoslovakia, the supreme commander having two equal-status deputies, one for FA and the other for PVO. The latter would control all aerospace defence forces, including all the gigantic mobile SAM/AAA forces previously an organic part of the 85 Ground-Force divisions (plus 64 combat-ready divisions in reserve in the adjoining area of the Soviet Union) in that TVD.

It is impossible to discuss the Soviet air threat out of context of the mobile war which is the central feature of Soviet planning against NATO. It is well known that the VGK hopes that by a single sustained thrust Soviet and WP ground forces would reach the Channel ports in 100 hours from moving over their start lines. The main thrusts, of which there would probably be several, would be backed up by numerous OMGs (Operational Manoeuvre Groups), which are self-contained high-speed raiding groups representing a direct resurrection of the Mobile Groups used by the Red Army in 1943-45. OMGs have recently been organised at both divisional and corps levels. Their tasks would include deep penetration, disruption of NATO rear areas and the securing of terrain for the main Soviet thrusts without the need for nuclear or CBW (chemical/biological warfare), though they are especially well trained in exploiting the chaos that would exist in NATO areas after the use of any of these weapons. At theatre level the air forces, both FA and PVO, are geared to the closest co-operation with the OMGs. Special reconnaissance and communications systems would keep the TVD staff fully in the picture in real time.

Several recent Western reports, and some by high-ranking Soviet writers, have emphasised the enormous spread of automation throughout the Soviet war machine. While there is only very little electronic data-processing in the civilian sector – so that this is one very large area where the Communist world lags many years behind the Free World, and is falling further behind daily – enormous sums have been spent on computer systems on the largest possible scale for the armed forces. As no comparable civilian systems exist, other than gradual introduction of an all-Union registration of details of the whole population, the military systems have been constructed from scratch, which has both advantages and disadvantages. The main advantage is probably that with totally central control it is possible to avoid problems of incompatibility of hardware, programming language or operator skills. Systems already handle the entire PVO aerospace defence. Other systems are being built for overall theatre warfare direction, inventory and stock control, personnel details, skills and assignments, and hardware maintenance, service record and spares provisioning.

As in more traditional aspects of the defence system, there is a sharp contrast between the colossal scale and sophistication of the military automation network in the Soviet Union and that in the satellite and client countries. The latter are poor relations by comparison.

To a fund-starved defender of the West, the way the Soviets spend money on war material often appears staggering. There are countless examples of instances where, though an existing item could readily have been used with small modifications, it has been decided to produce totally new designs just to get apparently trivial extra edges in performance or efficiency. Almost across the board, in weapons, EW and C^3, the policy has invariably been to do everything, and buy large numbers of all possible devices. For example, in the C^3 area the VVS and AVMF are furnished with airborne command posts, communications relay platforms and special surveillance platforms on a scale that would make any Western staff green with envy. Prolonged and widespread exercises in early 1983 tested the efficiency of eight types of manned C^3 aircraft (ranging from the Mi-8/Mi-17 up to the An-12, possibly in the variant known to NATO as 'Cub-B'), all operating together. Satellite communications were also involved. Airborne control was exercised at army, front, theatre and national levels, with the platforms in constant control with the ground and with each other by secure, jam-proof (believed digital, frequency hopping, spread-spectrum) radio links which are under computer control, to provide directional beaming where this can save effective radiated power, and also to record all signals for subsequent analysis. Staff in AVMF aircraft, including Tu-16s and Tu-142s, kept in touch with distant ballistic-missile submarines of the Baltic, Northern and Pacific fleets.

In the fundamental matter of technology most Western assessments rate the Soviet Union as hard-pressed to keep up with the West, except in specific military technology applications where their far greater effort – in money, manpower and material resources – has generally given it a lead. This is especially the case with EW, C^3 and computers, and the greatest technology gap of all is universally considered to lie in the field of directed energy. Though only marginally relevant to a book about traditional airpower, it is soon going to be of crucial importance because in any conflict with the Soviet Union after 1985 it is expected that NATO aircraft might be knocked out of the sky like flies by such weapons. The Soviet Union is known to have more than 60 large and highly classified facilities working in this field (which is maybe 55 more than in all NATO countries combined). There are three main branches: super-power lasers, super-power microwave generators and particle beams. Giant lasers are so far advanced in the Soviet Union that the official US Department of Defense view is that, 'The Soviets are committed to the development of specific laser weapon systems. Soviet development of moderate-power weapons capable of short-range ground-based applications such as tactical air defense and anti-personnel weapons may well be far enough along for such weapons to be fielded in the mid-1980s. In the latter half of this decade it is possible that the Soviets could produce laser weapons for several other ground, ship and aerospace applications.'

The Soviet Aircraft

Though the Soviet Union assigns General Aviation aircraft manufacture to the WP satellite countries, combat types are no longer permitted to be manufactured outside the Soviet Union. Thus all warplanes are standardised and come from the same Soviet production lines. The main Soviet designers and aircraft are detailed below.

Antonov

This design bureau was responsible for such important airlift transports as the An-12 ('Cub'), An-22 *Antei* ('Cock') and An-26 ('Curl'), and is now beginning production of the greatest aircraft in this class in the world. Believed to be the An-400, and called 'Condor' by NATO, this colossal machine outdoes the C-5 and is almost certainly the heaviest and most powerful aircraft of any kind in history. Long-range payload is 250tonne.

Beriev

This bureau concentrated on maritime aircraft. No replacement has appeared for the Be-12 ('Mail') turboprop amphibian used for ocean patrol, ASW and SAR/utility duties.

Ilyushin

As well as the very large Il-86 ('Camber') wide-bodied passenger transport, this bureau produces the Il-76 ('Candid') which is in use as an extremely important heavy transport and has been evaluated as the next-generation aircraft in two further important roles: inflight refuelling and AWACS (airborne early warning and control). The tanker was expected to enter service in 1983 equipped with three hose-drum units, thus providing the Soviet air forces with their first triple-point tanker. The AWACS version is generally supposed in the West to have flown with a rotodome above the rear fuselage as in the earlier Tu-126 'Moss', which was always regarded as an interim aircraft. Two things have now changed Soviet planning. One is the greatly superior antenna (aerial) configuration demonstrated by the RAF Nimrod AEW3, and the other is the development by the Ilyushin bureau of the very large Il-86 passenger transport which has much greater internal volume. The NATO opinion by 1984 was that the definitive Soviet AWACS will have nose and tail radomes on the Il-86 airframe. The existence of an Il-96 has been disclosed; this could be a re-engined Il-86 or possibly even the AWACS version.

MiG-21

Called 'Fishbed' by NATO, this exceedingly agile

Below:
For several reasons the Tu-126 ('Moss') needed replacement at an early date. The replacement appears to be this version of Il-76MD known to NATO as 'Mainstay', but in the longer term it is expected the Il-86 or Il-96 will be used as the basis for an aircraft with the more efficient nose/tail scanners.

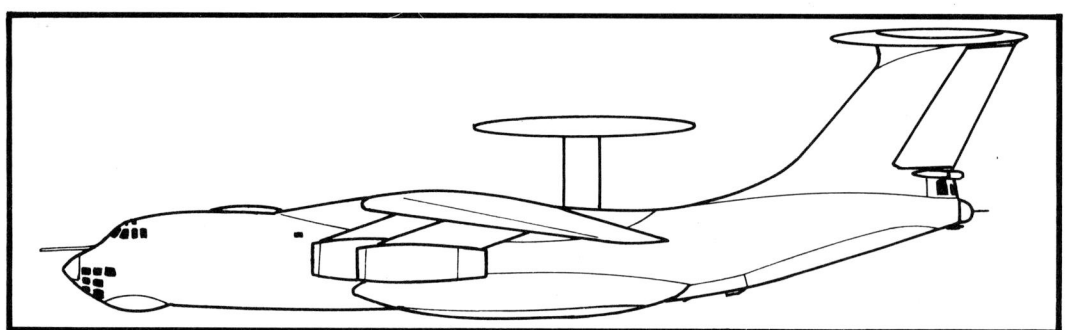

Top:
This MiG-21MF 'Fishbed-J' typifies an agile day fighter whose chief virtues are simplicity and good handling – and sheer numbers. Armament comprises a 23mm gun and a mix of short-range AAMs. *via J. W. R. Taylor*

Above:
Also photographed in East Germany, this MiG-27 'Flogger-D' is a member of the dedicated ground attack half of this prolific swing-wing family. Its engine is as powerful as that of the MiG-23, the take off thrust being 25,350lb, but its inlets and nozzle are simplified for low-level, mainly subsonic, operation. *MoD*

tailed delta is still in service in very large numbers and in many versions, though these are being replaced. By far their most important task is establishing daylight air superiority, using search and lock-on radar and close-range missiles and guns, backed up by the usual comprehensive EW and IFF systems. Though limited by short mission endurance and small weapon load, the MiG-21 is formidable in the dogfight role and probably has an advantage because of its massive numerical superiority. The full spectrum of weapons is not known, but includes AA-2 'Atoll', AA-2-2 'Advanced Atoll' and AA-8 'Aphid' missiles, as well as various gun installations, the usual internal gun being the GSh-23 cannon with 200 rounds. Reconnaissance models generally fly unarmed, but all versions can carry air/ground stores on underwing pylons (usually four).

MiG-23/27

Called 'Flogger' by NATO, this family of single-engined swing-wing aircraft is believed to be being built at a rate exceeding all other combat aircraft in the world, Western estimates being in the

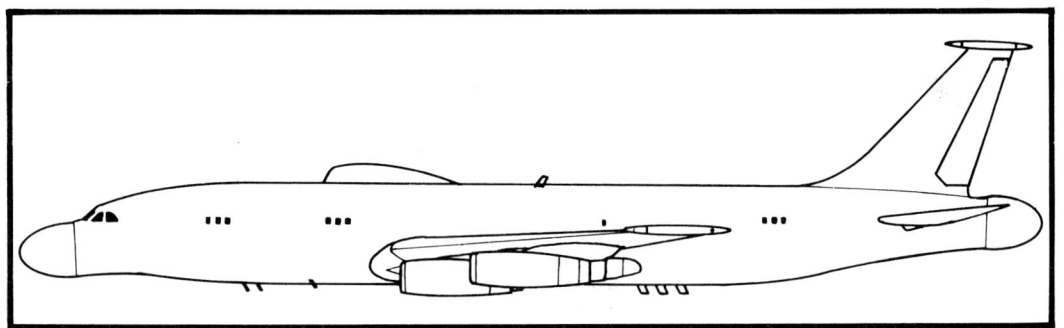

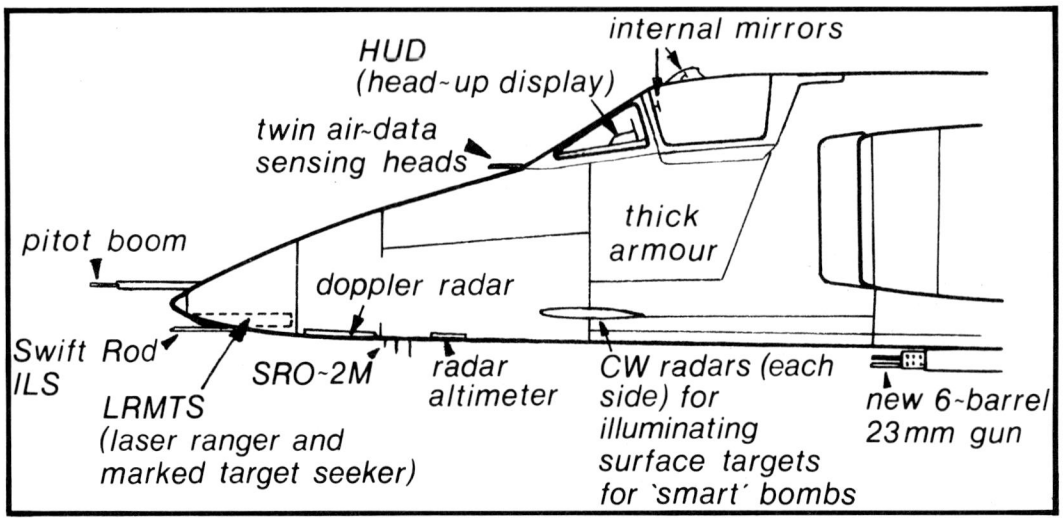

HUD
(head-up display)

internal mirrors

twin air-data
sensing heads

thick
armour

pitot boom

doppler radar

Swift Rod
ILS

SRO-2M

radar
altimeter

LRMTS
(laser ranger and
marked target seeker)

CW radars (each
side) for
illuminating
surface targets
for 'smart' bombs

new 6-barrel
23mm gun

Above:

In service in daunting numbers, the MiG-23BN and MiG-27 are specialised attack aircraft whose front end might serve as a model for others to copy. All it lacks are a multimode radar, perfect all-round pilot view and a modern cockpit.

range 50 to 70 aircraft per month. Total deliveries by early 1984 were estimated at 3,600, exclusive of exports outside the WP. There are two basic sub-families, one (based on the MiG-23MF) being an all-weather interceptor and air-superiority fighter, and the other (based on the MiG-23BN and MiG-27) being a dedicated ground-attack aircraft. Both have a single extremely powerful afterburning turbojet, but while the attack model has simple fixed inlets and a short nozzle, the fighter has fully modulated inlets and nozzle for maximum supersonic performance at all heights. This engine installation is one of the chief differences between the families, the other being the nose. The MiG-23MF has a fighter nose with a low-drag cockpit with interception displays fed by a large multimode radar and extremely comprehensive SIF/IFF and fighter type EW installations, as well as CW guidance for radar-homing missiles. The attack model has a high-mounted cockpit with the best possible forward view (surprisingly obstructed by a mass of mirrors, sights and pitot heads) over a 'ducknose' which slopes sharply down to a flat tip packed with air-to-ground sensors and weapon-delivery systems which do not include any forward-looking radar. Heavy armour plate protects the pilot from fire directed from below. Both aircraft are to a considerable degree multirole, and in fact there are intermediate versions with the fighter powerplant installation and attack nose. Avionic equipment is evidently extremely

comprehensive, and in true Soviet style these aircraft are tough and delightful to fly. Despite the absence of pylons on the pivoting wings, there is no shortage of warload. The MF carries a GSh-23 gun and typically two giant AA-7 'Apex' missiles and two or four small AA-8 'Aphid' dogfight missiles, plus a 176gal centreline tank to augment the excellent internal capacity of 1,265gal (1,520 US gal, 5,750 litres). The attack versions usually have a new six-barrel gun, believed to fire the standard 23mm ammunition but at rates up to 4,000 rounds/min, and tandem twin or quad ejector racks for 16 FAB-250 bombs (total 4tonne, 8,820lb) or various other loads up to 5tonne for short ranges. Front-line units of the FA and Aviation Armies have over 1,600 of both versions, while the PVO has over 500 of the interceptor. Shortcomings include poor rearward view, and in the fighter a generally unimpressive thrust/weight ratio and turn capability (because at high weights the wing loading is high) and lack of a really fully developed look-down shoot-down capability. A carrier-based version is expected to equip the 60,000ton carrier now building.

MiG-25/31
Called 'Foxbat' by NATO, the MiG-25 caused alarm when it appeared (together with a string of world speed records) in 1965. Entering service as an interceptor in 1970, and as a multisensor reconnaissance aircraft a year later, the MiG-25 has always been a unique aircraft, extremely large, basically simple and by brute force and good design able to outrun all other combat aircraft in the world, though the unarmed SR-71 reconnaissance platform is faster. Working up to Mach 2.8 (or over Mach 3 without missiles) takes time, burns a vast amount of fuel and prohibits any kind of manoevrability. There is no place for the MiG-25 over the European

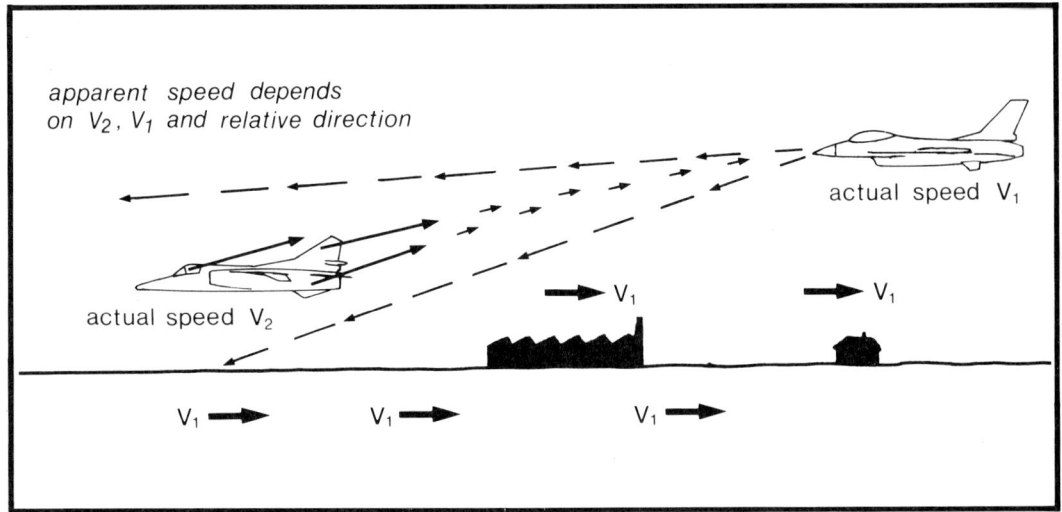

Above:

Look-down shoot-down radar, and associated radar-guided missiles, rely for their operation entirely upon being able by doppler frequency measurement to differentiate between the land surface and a target moving at a different relative speed just above it. A little thought will show that low-flying aircraft might escape detection by crossing the interceptor's path at such a relative angle that it would have the same relative speed as the ground below it; clever radars can still detect the target from the land surface.

Left:

Known to NATO as 'Foxbat-E', the current all-weather interceptor version of the MiG-25 has limited look-down shoot-down capability. It also probably has uprated engines each of 30,865lb thrust and various other improvements. In turn, 'Foxbat-E' is giving way to the MiG-31 'Foxhound'. *US DoD*

Below:

By 1984 the MiG-31 'Foxhound' was reported in the Department of Defense to equip at least four air regiments. A longer two-seat version of the MiG-25 'Foxbat', the MiG-31 has new radar, eight AA-9 long-range missiles and unrivalled stand-off kill capability.

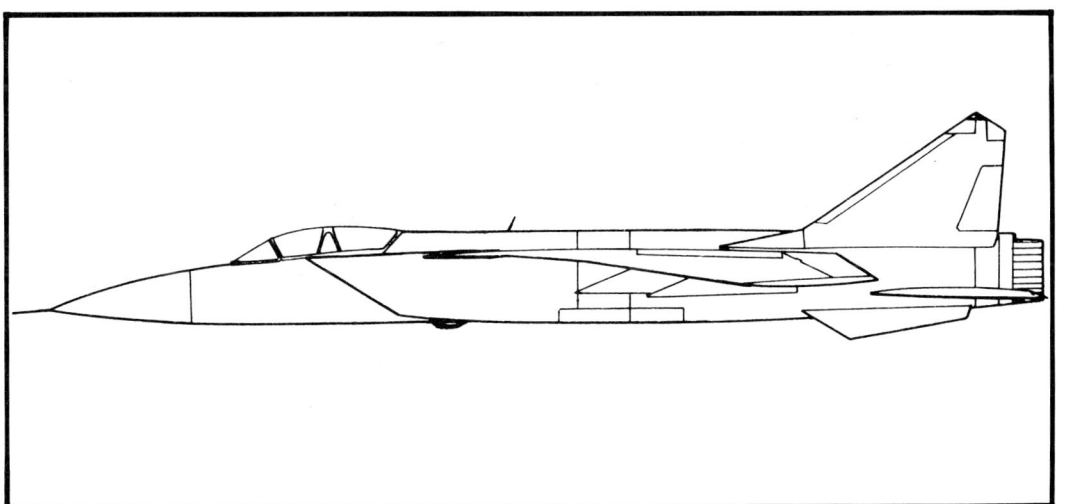

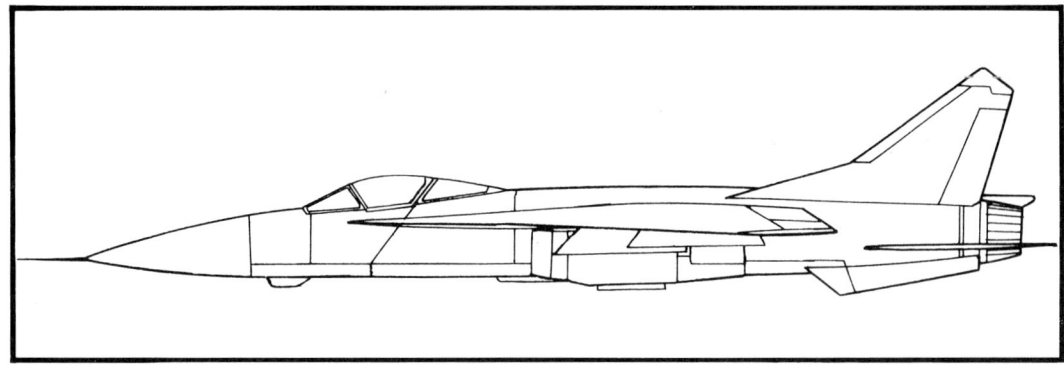

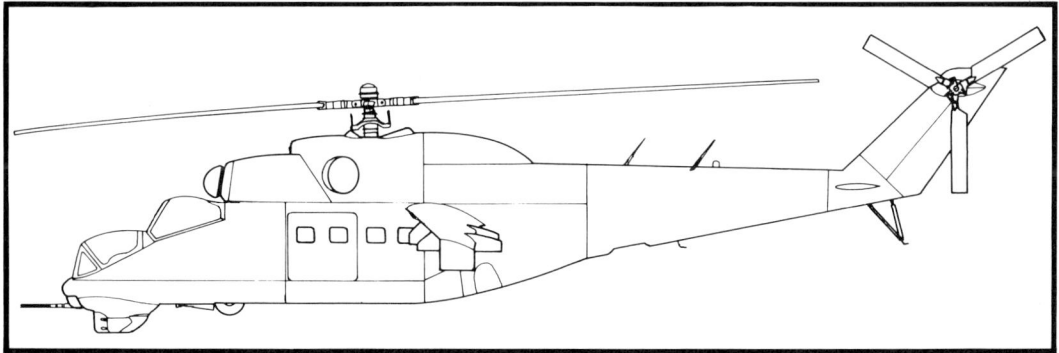

Top:
There is no longer any doubt that the MiG-29 'Fulcrum' has a long-range TWS (track while scan) pulse-doppler radar with full look-down shoot-down capability, as well as additional IR (infra-red) search and track, both sensors feeding TV-type and head-up displays. It has a gun and six AAMs.

Above:
The Mi-24 is an extremely fast helicopter which in all its versions has a large cabin for a squad of troops or other internal loads. Possibly the new Mi-28 is the same helicopter with the gunship front end, and with the cabin deleted.

battle area, except possibly with considerable EW support as a stand-off killer of AWACS and EF-111A type aircraft, using IR-homing or radar-homing missiles larger than any others in the world. The MiG-25MP ('Foxbat E') is an improved model with a strengthened airframe and various avionic and weapon changes tailored to countering low-altitude threats, which is something the original 'Foxbat A' could not do. It is believed that most or all of this low-level version are rebuilds. Since 1982 the Aviation Armies and possibly the PVO have begun receiving a true second-generation interceptor derived from the MiG-25, the MiG-31 ('Foxhound'). Described as 'the first Soviet interceptor with true look-down/shoot-down capability', and further assessed in the last chapter, the MiG-31 is an impressive machine which matches the speed of the MiG-25 with far greater

versatility, more weapons and formidable manoeuvrability (though not equal to the MiG-29) from a large and quite different wing.

MiG-29

Called 'Fulcrum' by NATO, this is the most agile fighter in the Soviet armoury, and possibly in the world. Western experts who have seen it on film have been deeply impressed, and not a little concerned, at its all-round performance and amazing manoeuvrability. As far back as 1981 artist's impressions were appearing in the West, showing a cross between an F/A-18A and a MiG-25, but smaller and lighter than either. There is no doubt the true appearance has yet to emerge,

Right:
In most respects the Soviet Mi-24 family of helicopters are the most formidable in large-scale service anywhere in the world. All models have the unusual attribute of combining attack or anti-tank weapons with a cabin for a squad of troops or other load. This is the anti-armour version called 'Hind-D' by NATO.

Far right:
Originally designed as a large short-range fighter to intercept USAF 'Century series' fighter-bombers, the Sukhoi Su-7 matured in the late 1950s as a day attack aircraft carrying a limited load of bombs or rockets. Its main attributes are amazing toughness and superb handling at all speeds. This Su-7BM, the oldest type in use, serves with the Czech CL.

and it could well be found to have a foreplane or even vectoring nozzles. Twin-engined, it has a fixed-sweep (indeed, almost unswept) wing with variable camber for sustained violent turns; and there is evidence it has CCV qualities and can translate laterally or vertically without change of attitude. The primary role is all-weather air combat, using look-down/shoot-down BVR (beyond visual range) missiles. Thrust/weight ratio is possibly 1.5 in the clean condition, and it remains above unity in all low-level configurations, giving truly remarkable performance akin to that planned for the original light F-16. Curiously, the Department of Defense also describes this aircraft as having 'improved range', compared with earlier fighters, despite the very high T/W ratio. Full-scale service is predicted for 'the late 1980s', though why an aircraft tested in quantity prior to 1980 should need such a long gestation is not explained. One may expect heavy air/ground weapon loads to be an alternative to air combat weapons. (In September 1984 Western reports claimed the MiG-29 was in deep trouble with engines and radar; there is no evidence to support these stories.)

Mi-24

In general helicopters are not dealt with here, but the Mi-24 (NATO name, 'Hind') is so important its presence to the tune of 900 examples (including a few 'Hip-E' armed Mi-8s) opposite NATO in Europe must be recorded. Able to carry 11 to 13 armed troops in its cabin, the Mi-24 exists in several versions, some of which have a gunship nose packed with navigation and weapon-aiming sensors, the weapons including the usual mass of 57mm rockets and also advanced anti-tank missiles and a multi-barrel 12.7mm turreted nose gun or side packs with GSh-23s. Army Aviation was established in 1982 to enable air power to become an organic part of the Soviet Ground Forces, and six Mi-24s are now on strength with the air squadron of every ground-force division. The prolonged and brutal war in Afghanistan has been very useful in proving hardware and techniques, notably including

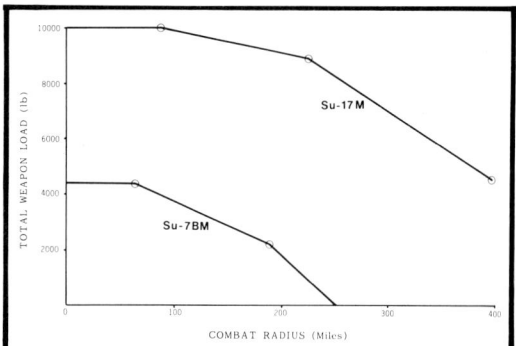

Above:
Thanks to the introduction of swing-wings the rather ineffectual – though immensely tough and popular – Su-7 series has been transformed in capability and retained in production almost up to the present.

chemical attacks and close collaboration between attack helicopters and fixed-wing machines such as the Su-25.

Su-7/-17/-22

The original Su-7 went into production as long ago as 1958 as a standard FA close-support attack aircraft. Almost as big and powerful as an F-105, this tailed, acutely swept, mid-wing machine was from the start popular because of its great toughness and beautiful handling (though pilots soon became tired from the heavy control forces). On the other hand it accomplished little with its big and thirsty engine, and it was commonly said the Su-7 could carry fuel or bombs but not both at once. Later versions introduced good off-airfield capability, a clean aircraft demonstrating use of a 400m (1,300ft) sod strip, but all these early models have now been supplanted in front-line WP service by the swing-wing Su-17 and Su-22 families which, despite having only the small outermost part of the wing pivoted, have a bombload increased from 2tonne (with twin drop tanks) to 5tonne, yet have a

mission radius increased by 30%! Between 1971 and 1981 nine further improved versions entered service with a new engine, far more comprehensive avionics and greatly increased lethality. All are just supersonic at sea level in the clean condition, and with a typical bombload of 4tonne can still exceed 500mph (800km/hr) and make an accurate blind attack on terrain-following radar and using a HUD and laser ranger. Almost 1,000 swing-wing versions are in WP service. They all carry one or two of the same devastating 30mm guns as fitted to the Su-7, but air-combat capability is limited.

Below:
Called 'Fencer' by NATO, the Sukhoi Su-24 long range interdiction aircraft is an outstandingly formidable machine possessed of tremendous flight performance despite colossal internal (and if necessary external) fuel capacity. It can be thought of as either a scaled-up Tornado or as a new-generation F-111. It probably has the highest wing-loading of any combat aircraft, making for a smooth low-level ride at maximum sweep.

Below right:
This is a different Su-24, with many details contrasting with those of the aircraft in the picture (*Below*). Though the wings are again at minimum sweep, the slats, flaps and landing gear are retracted.

Su-9/-11

These single-engined delta interceptors were at one time very numerous in the PVO, but none remains opposite NATO in central Europe. They never served with satellite forces.

Su-15

Though derived from the single-engined family just mentioned, this next-generation series of twin-jet interceptors has been greatly developed and even today remains extremely formidable. Like most PVO aircraft the Su-15, called 'Flagon' by NATO, is tailored to long paved runways, allowing it to have a very high wing loading. This reduces dogfight manoeuvrability, but the Su-15 is, like the MiG-25, a stand-off all-weather killer, and tailored to high speed, fast climb and the very best kit of avionics and weapons. All versions in service have an extended-span wing with a planform almost resembling the MiG-31, and a very long fuselage housing most of the fuel, the twin turbojet engines and a very large radar which in the latest version has look-down/shoot-down capability (this is being retrofitted in earlier aircraft). Originally the only missile was the big AA-3 'Anab', and like almost all PVO all-weather interceptors it has always been usual to carry one with semi-active radar homing and one with infra-red guidance to increase the certainty of a kill no matter what the ambient

Possessed of a tremendous flight performance, the Sukhoi Su-15 has been progressively improved and is seen here in the current version, with comprehensive radar and EW systems. It is carrying two AA-3 'Anab' large AAMs and two dogfight AA-8 'Aphid' AAMs (whose true designation is R-60). The two belly-mounted gun pods are not installed on this occasion. *Swedish Air Force*

conditions or enemy countermeasures. Since 1980 the twin body pylons, which are plumbed for drop tanks, have been used to carry AA-2 or AA-8 dogfight missiles or twin 23mm gun pods. These guns were used in 1983 to fire at the South Korean Boeing 747 before it was shot down by an 'Anab'.

Su-24

Known to NATO personnel as 'Fencer', this long-range interdiction aircraft is almost a WP counterpart of the F-111. Its design was very strongly influenced by the US aircraft, even to the very questionable point of having side-by-side seating, but it avoided the more obvious shortcomings of the F-111 in having long inlet ducts and a wide belly able to carry a heavy weapon load whilst leaving the wing pylons still available for tanks or jammer pods. A much closer description would be to call the Su-24 the WP Tornado, but in comparison with that aircraft it is very much bigger, heavier and more powerful; the gross weight is roughly 50% greater and the engine power getting on for 70% greater. For the first time on a production Soviet aircraft there are swivelling pylons under the outer wings, the normal maximum bombload (no tanks or ECM pods) being eight pylons each with a one-tonne rating, a total of 17,635lb. Naturally this aircraft is packed with every modern avionic device for all-weather terrain-following at very low level, precise blind navigation, penetration of heavily defended hostile airspace, and precision delivery of a wide range of weapons. At weights up to about 60,000lb (27.2tonne), the clean gross weight, operations are possible from unpaved airstrips of 800m (2,625ft) length. In the attack role this aircraft has no superior in the world, and since 1975 output has been at about the rate of 100 per year. Most examples seen in FA (now AASU) service have two belly blisters which may be guns of different types, though one has been identified as a combined FLIR/laser installation for ultra-precise air-to-ground weapon aiming. It is believed that four types of air-to-ground guided missile can be carried (AS-7, -9, -11 and -12) though little is known about these weapons. For self-defence AA-2, AA-2-2 and AA-8 can be carried (often on twin launchers), but these costly aircraft would certainly not seek combat. Protection against AA fire is certain to be

of a high order, and one possible reason for side-by-side seating may be the reduced weight of armour needed with this cockpit arrangement. Other versions exist, believed to include dedicated reconnaissance, EW and possibly interceptor variants, but none has yet (1984) been positively identified in service.

Su-25

Called 'Frogfoot' by NATO, this close-support machine was obviously triggered by the USAF A-10A, and like that machine trades speed for weapon load and good protection against hostile fire. It would be hard to imagine a more conventional aircraft, with a configuration actually similar to the Northrop A-9A, the A-10's losing rival. A single-seater, the Su-25 carries a weapon load of at least 8tonne (17,635lb) on 10 pylons, and is almost certainly built around a gun of tremendous power used against tanks and other hard-skinned targets. An obviously inaccurate DoD artist's impression published in 1983 showed nose radar, a MiG-23 type canopy flush with the top of the fuselage and variable (afterburner type) engine nozzles, but these features are at variance with photographs taken in 1982 in Afghanistan, where these aircraft have proved deadly to thousands of defenders. Obviously there must be adequate weapon-aiming systems, but there is no evidence that these are any more comprehensive than the austere kit fitted to the A-10A and tailored to attacks in visual conditions. On the other hand, the

Below:
Prepared by a US Department of Defense artist, this sketch of the Sukhoi Su-25, or 'Frogfoot', is the only clear illustration at present available, though it certainly differs in many respects from the true aircraft as seen in fuzzy ciné film. *DoD*

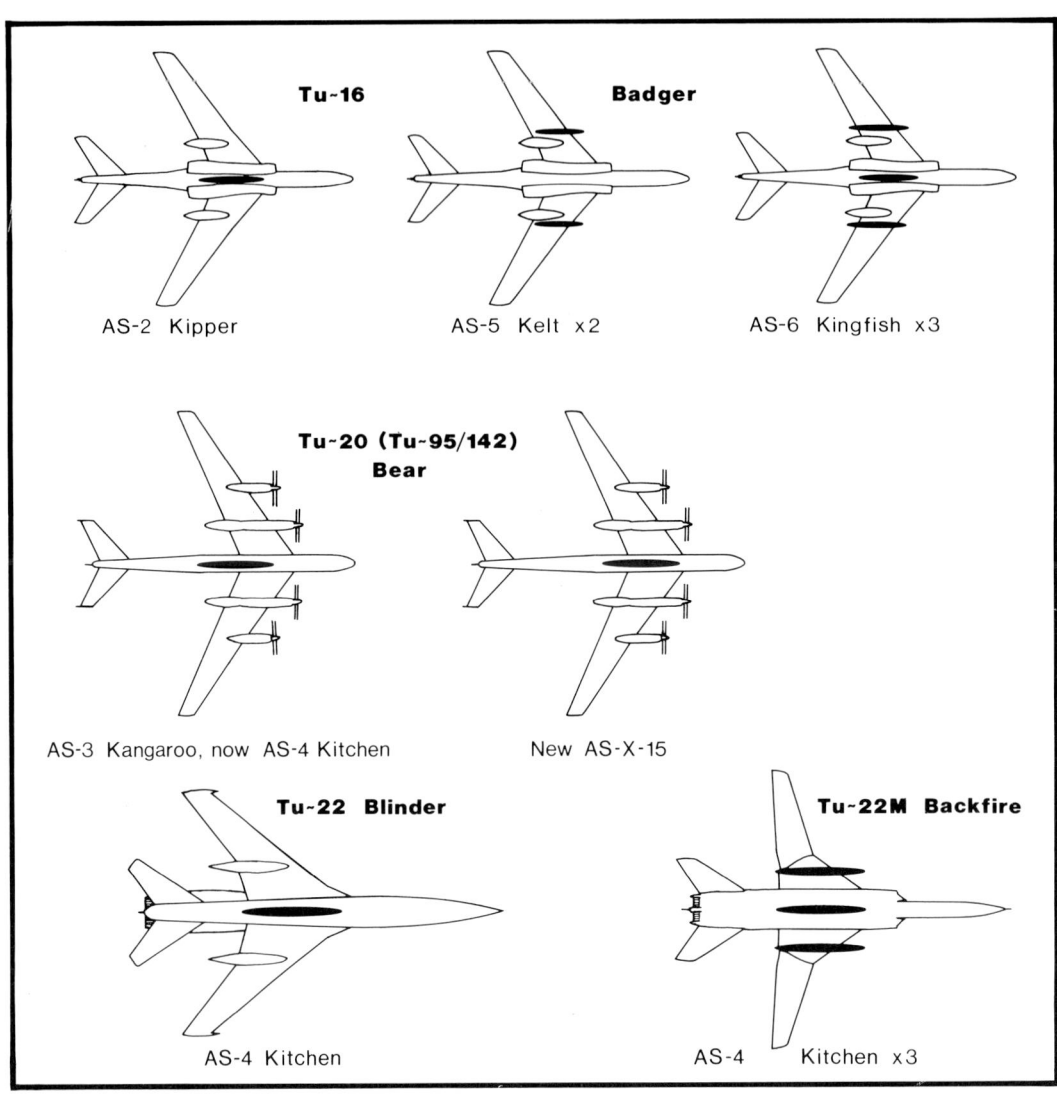

Tu-16   **Badger**

AS-2 Kipper   AS-5 Kelt x2   AS-6 Kingfish x3

Tu-20 (Tu-95/142)
Bear

AS-3 Kangaroo, now AS-4 Kitchen   New AS-X-15

Tu-22 Blinder   **Tu-22M Backfire**

AS-4 Kitchen   AS-4   Kitchen x3

available photographs suggest an extremely comprehensive EW capability, including equipment for countering radar and IR missiles fired from the ground or air. Afghan experience has refined tactics in which Su-25s and Mi-24s work together, using conventional and chemical weapons, to destroy people trying to shelter in the most rugged rocky terrain. Different methods would be needed on NATO's Central Front, where the Su-25 had not appeared by late 1983. Afghanistan was ideal for it, but in Western Europe this aircraft might prove less effective and more vulnerable.

Su-27
Called 'Flanker' by NATO, this extremely advanced multirole fighter is clearly very formidable, but by late 1983 so little was known about it that comment could be misleading. From

1981 (when it was just called 'Ram-J', meaning 'Type J' seen at Ramenskoye test base) this fighter has been described as in the class of the F-14 and F-15, meaning that it is twin-engined and highly supersonic. Early reports of a swing wing now appear less confident. The 1983 DoD assessment merely commented that this is one of the key look-down/shoot-down/BVR fighters with which the Soviet forces expect to gain rapid and total air superiority at the start of any major campaign. In timing it is running later than the MiG-29 and -31, and is not expected in service until the middle of the decade. Further comments appear in the last chapter.

Tu-16
The familiar 'Badger' has been in service for 30 years, and though very long in the tooth remains in

Known as 'Flanker' to NATO, the extremely formidable Su-27 long-range all-weather multirole fighter is expected to become operational in 1985, a year later than the MiG-29. Carrying eight AAMs, or at least 12 bombs of 1,102lb (500kg) each, the Su-27 is said to be ready in a naval version for the giant new Soviet carrier, expected to be named *Kremlin.*

Left:
No other country has anything remotely like the variety, size and numbers of the long-range cruise missiles carried by Soviet bombers (not to scale). In most cases the original version was for use against ships. Range of the AS-X-15 is over 1,864 miles (3,000km).

service in such numbers (over 480), and doing so many tasks, that it is still important. Missions include free-fall bombing (conventional, nuclear and chemical), ECM high-power jamming, Elint, multisensor reconnaissance, inflight-refuelling tanker and air-to-surface missile delivery.

Tu-20/-95/-142
Commonly called 'Bear', this family of enormous strategic platforms remains unique in combining jet speed with propeller propulsion, the latter combining with the long-span wing to give exceptional range and endurance. In 1983 these were the only aircraft representing a direct nuclear manned threat to the USA, almost all of which could be reached in a two-way mission. The six current variants comprise three for strike (one free-fall bomber and two with missiles), two for strategic reconnaissance, and the totally revised Tu-142 anti-submarine version which was still being produced new in early 1983. The DoD estimated that 113 of the basic bomber type were operational in 1983, plus about 100 of other models and over 50 Tu-142s with the AVMF. In 1984 it was discovered that a new version, Bear-H, is also being built from scratch to carry the AS-X-15 long range missile.

Tu-22/-22M
Called 'Blinder' by NATO, the Tu-22 was the first Soviet supersonic bomber to go into production, in 1962. Though having only two engines, this machine is 133ft (over 40.5m) long and can weigh 85tonne (187,500lb) with full internal fuel, giving a

tactical radius, including a 250-mile (400km) low-level supersonic dash, of 1,750 miles (2,800km). Ferry range on internal fuel is estimated at 4,040 miles (6,500km). About 200 were built, and these are deployed as free-fall bombers, air-to-surface missile carriers, multisensor reconnaissance and trainer aircraft. It was estimated that 140 were combat-ready for bomber/reconnaissance missions opposite NATO in 1983, forming (says the DoD) 'a potent force' when operating with 'Badger' and 'Backfire'. The latter aircraft, the Tu-22M in its original form, was derived from the Tu-22 by adding pivoting outer wings and other changes, but it grew into a largely new aircraft with different engine installations, even greater fuel capacity and inward-retracting main landing gears. Though the Soviet Union insisted during SALT talks that it was only a theatre aircraft, rather than an intercontinental one, and childishly removed the inflight-refuelling probes for a time in support of this contention, the fact remains that operating from several Siberian Arctic bases the regular aircraft can cover a substantial part of the USA on internal fuel, and with inflight refuelling can take in the entire USA and most of Mexico. Missions are nuclear and conventional strike, anti-ship and reconnaissance, and more important than its highly supersonic performance at height is a range of low-level penetration features which make it much more survivable than its predecessors. About 150 serve with the 30th and 36th Air Armies, while about the same number are operational with the AVMF, usually with a recessed AS-4 'Kitchen' stand-off missile or two AS-6 'Kingfish' missiles under the wings. All these weapons can approach their target from any direction, on any flight profile, and have a large nuclear or conventional warhead. What is more surprising is that some AVMF aircraft have been seen with long external racks for a large number of conventional stores including free-fall bombs. Similar racks may be used from about 1985 when an ALCM with a predicted range of 1,864 miles (3,000km) becomes operational. This weapon, say the DoD, will 'provide the Soviets with greatly improved capabilities for low-level and standoff attack in both theatre and intercontinental operations'.

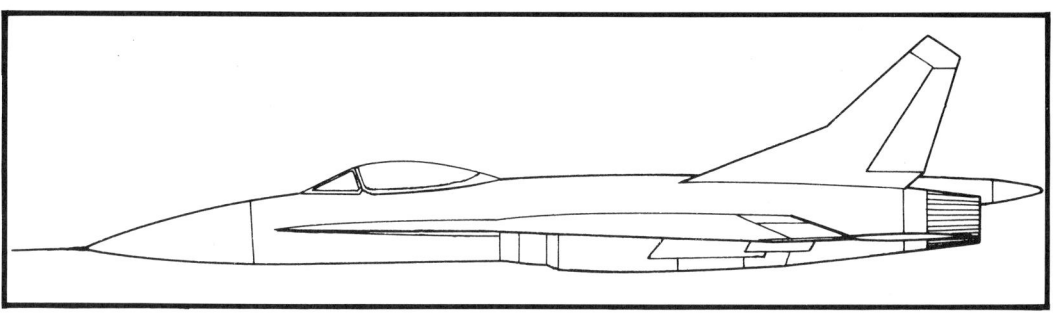

'Blackjack'

Previously called 'Ram-P', this extremely large swing-wing bomber strongly resembles the USAF B-1 in layout but is appreciably larger. It will presumably be equipped for inflight refuelling, but even without it will be able to cover targets throughout the entire Northern Hemisphere while carrying a very heavy load of nuclear or conventional free-fall bombs or stand-off missiles. Though prototypes have been on test since 1979 this formidable aircraft is not expected to be operational until about 1986.

Yak-28

The numerous variants of this tactical twin-jet are being phased out of front-line service, though a few Yak-28P interceptors continue with the PVO. The chief duty of those ready for action is high-power jamming and other EW tasks.

Yak-36MP

Called 'Forger' by NATO, this trim vectored-thrust VTOL is carried by the four units of the 37,000ton 'Kiev' class ships. Often called an attack aircraft by the DoD, it also flies interception missions with AA-8 missiles and gun pods, or reconnaissance missions with a multisensor fuselage pack mounted ventrally.

Below:
One of the greatest of all military aircraft, the amazing aircraft of the Tupolev family called 'Bear' by NATO are the fastest propeller machines ever built and have also served on very challenging missions for almost 30 years. This Tu-95 'Bear-D' is one of a sub-species with the tail turret replaced by a long fairing. It is not certain if the pressurised tail crew compartment is retained.

Bottom:
The impressive long-range 'Backfire', to which the Soviet SALT 2 negotiators gave the designation Tu-22M, now operates in formidable strength all over the northern hemisphere. This example has the usual triple tandem external racks, but its probe has been removed. *Royal Danish AF*

The NATO Ground Defences

In the first chapter the point was made that any country threatened with invasion by an enemy equipped with vastly superior airpower ought to invest very heavily indeed in air-defence systems comprising a computer-linked radar network plus the greatest possible number of SAM launchers with at least a dozen reload missiles for each launcher. Such investment would be likely to defeat anything the enemy could do in the air, leaving his land forces to press forward with no support from the sky.

Possibly, at this point, our hypothetical

defending country could then bring out its own, previously well hidden, airpower and attack the enemy ground forces. But such cosy scenarios are likely in practice to come unstuck for various reasons. Certainly the NATO response to the

Below:
Thanks to unbroken high-rate production the Soviet Union has been able to provide itself and its allies with airpower for a fraction of the price paid by the divisive West. Whatever happens, Western Europe must soon decide on its single multinational fighter for the 1990s.

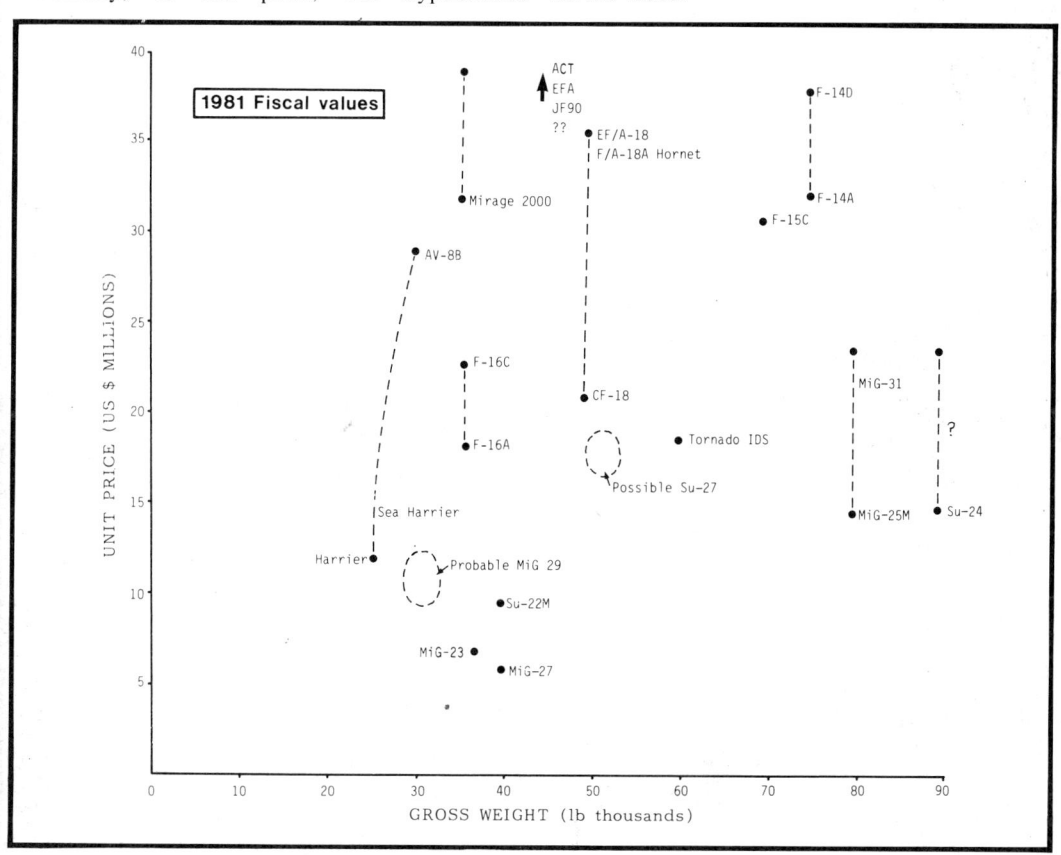

growing might of the Warsaw Pact air forces has been to try to build up its own air forces, but this is an uphill struggle.

First, it is simply not possible to attempt to match the Soviet Union's rate of output, even though combat aircraft are no longer permitted to be manufactured in any WP country except the Soviet Union. The Soviet aircraft industry has been further expanded in recent years, in contrast to the continuing reductions in almost every NATO aerospace company. According to the US Department of Defense in 1983: 'New, large final-assembly buildings have been built at nearly every established plant. A wholly new, large, aircraft plant is under construction. This plant, when completed, will probably be used to fabricate and assemble large aircraft – transports and bombers. Qualitative improvements in production technology, which typically accompany new and more sophisticated aircraft, have paralleled the physical growth of the industry.'

These increases in productive capacity have further improved the Soviet Union's already very large advantage over the West in unit cost. Obviously, precise details of Soviet manufacturing costs are not publicly known in the West, but the information given in the accompanying graphical plot of aircraft prices is an educated guess which has been agreed by several Western authorities as a fair compromise. It will be seen that, because of relatively low production rates, high labour costs and inflation, the prices of all NATO aircraft other than the F-16 are far higher than those for the most important Soviet aircraft.

Thus the ideal NATO response, of gearing the efforts of the 15 united members of the Alliance to produce common hardware, continues to prove a pipe-dream. This, however, should not be the case. Far from the Soviet Union and WP countries being able to dominate NATO, the reverse should be true if population and GNP (Gross National Product) are any guide. NATO has far more people, and far more money and resources, than the aggregate for the WP countries. But only a little of it is applied to military ends, and few people in NATO would wish this to change – however great the threat. What is surely tragic is that the very limited funding is frittered away on a multiplicity of duplicative programmes which, despite 30 years of pious talking, are often not interoperable and in many cases are even mutually incompatible.

Nowhere is the need for a single integrated system more obviously needed than in the matter of defence against air or missile attack. So far NATO had done little against missiles, the only ABM (anti-ballistic missile) system being the US Safeguard, which was deactivated on the same day (1 October 1975) that the first site was activated. Since then the West, unlike the Soviet Union, not

only has had no defence against ballistic missiles but has no plans to provide any such defence. (The Soviet Union, on the other hand, pours money into anti-missile defence, and not only are large 'farms' of silo-emplaced interceptor missiles being built on a wide scale but the new Pushkino radars are the largest in existence.)

The absence of any NATO defence against any type of Warsaw Pact ballistic missile is curious, and disquieting. Such weapons, with any of four types of warhead – conventional, nuclear, chemical or biological – pose an extremely serious threat to every fixed NATO installation, including every airfield. There is no doubt that this threat has frequently been discussed by NATO organisations from the Military Committee down, but so far there has been no announcement of any action being taken – not even a study programme. This contrasts with the US national outlay for missile warning to protect its own strategic deterrent, currently running at $830million annually.

This absence of any anti-missile defence is central to this chapter, because it places at risk everything in NATO whose position is known, and this includes virtually all the NATO fixed-wing aircraft. Even the RAF's four combat-ready squadrons of Harriers, which have been thus equipped for 14 years, can be caught at their home airfields on almost every day of the year except on the few days when they are detached for an exercise. These aircraft could, at least, be made survivable by dispersal, though carrying conventional ordnance they are so few in number the 85 WP divisions in the territories immediately adjacent to NATO would hardly regard them as more than a pin-prick.

Thus, for this chapter to be meaningful we must first make the nonsensical assumption that the missiles targeted at NATO's fixed installations would remain in their launchers! In other words, that the Soviet commanders would decide to use only the weapons against which NATO has defences, which is precisely how they would *not*

passive role, as does Iceland, and both leave their chairs empty at all military meetings (though for administrative reasons the only 'NATO' aircraft, the 18 E-3A Sentry AWACS aircraft, are registered in the former country). Thus, with rare exceptions only 13 nations make an active contribution to the Alliance, though in a few programmes the total is 14 because of participation by France. The point must also be made that, as by far the most powerful member of the Alliance, the USA took a significant step when it created the idea of an RDF (Rapid Deployment Force), able to rush combat-ready forces of various kinds to any trouble spot. Though intended primarily for snuffing out 'brushfire' conflicts elsewhere, the RDF would play an active and possibly crucial role in any conflict between WP forces and NATO nations in Europe. Substantial infrastructure (fixed installations) has recently been created providing ready-stocked stores for RDF use in emergency, though almost all NATO infrastructure funding is running years behind programme and is fast approaching a crisis point.

Passive defence

In the entire history of NATO there is just one shining example of a single integrated system to which all active members of the Alliance (ie, all except Iceland) have contributed. This system is NADGE (NATO Air Defence Ground Environment). By 1960 it was obvious that aircraft coming in from the east at treetop height at Mach 0.9, reaching their targets within minutes, could not effectively be countered by a defence network based on World War 2 practice, with some plotting centres still using large tables on which model aircraft were pushed around by human hands. Moreover, all the systems were national ones, often using ancient hardware such as 1944-vintage radars, and with many severe problems at the interfaces, which in the main followed the national frontiers and frequently involved communication via ordinary post office telephones!

For once, NATO spoke with (almost) one voice,

react in a real war. There are abundant articles appearing all the time in the Soviet military press explaining how they would actually play to win, by the most effective means.

Assuming, then, that NATO's installations remain undestroyed, there are three main methods to blunt WP air assault. One is passive defence, using camouflage, HASs (hardened aircraft shelters), going underground, dispersal (to the limited extent possible when units are based on airfields) and the use of electronic, infra-red (IR) and other techniques, such as barrage balloons, to interfere with enemy navigation and weapon delivery. The other two methods are both active: shooting down hostile aircraft, the only methods currently available being SAMs and AAA, and counter-air attack to attempt to destroy enemy aircraft on their airfields.

Not all NATO nations play an active role in defence; for example Luxembourg normally plays a

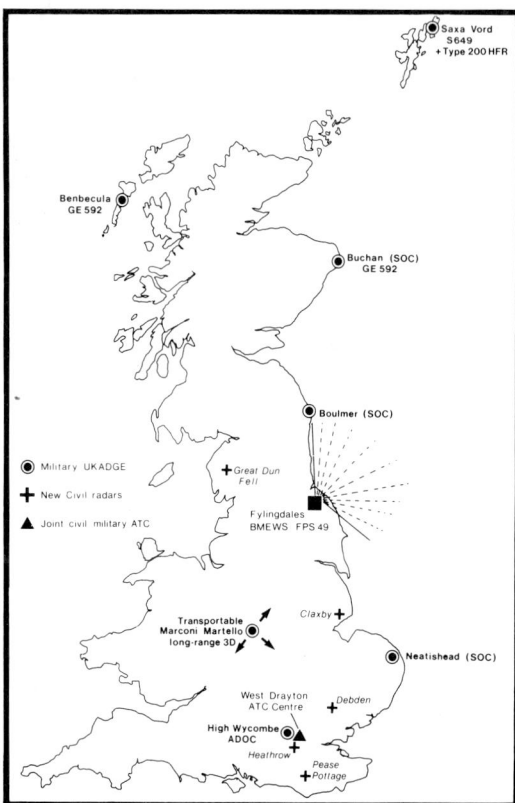

Benbecula
GE 592

Saxa Vord
S649
+ Type 200 HFR

Buchan (SOC)
GE 592

Boulmer (SOC)

◉ Military UKADGE

✛ New Civil radars

▲ Joint civil military ATC

✛ Great Dun
Fell

Fylingdales
BMEWS FPS 49

Transportable
Marconi Martello ◉
long-range 3D

Claxby ✛

Neatishead (SOC)

West Drayton
ATC Centre
Debden ✛

High Wycombe ◉▲
ADOC

Heathrow

Pease
✛ Pottage

Above:
**To attempt a comprehensive map of UKADGE
would be to transgress security, but this shows
some of the main centres together with the chief
surveillance radars installed. HFR is heightfinder
radar, SOC Sector Operations Centre and ADOC
Air-Defence Operations Centre.**

and it was agreed to create a single unified system
using state-of-the-art hardware forming a totally
compatible defence net from North Cape, in
northern Norway, sweeping in a giant curve
through Scandinavia and Central Europe and then
on through Italy and Greece to the thousand-mile
length of Turkey, ending on the summit of the
Bible's Mount Ararat where the white golfballs of
the surveillance radars look far into the Soviet
Union. By any yardstick, NADGE was a most
impressive achievement.

It was managed and constructed by a
multinational company, Nadgeco, whose HQ was,
improbably, tucked above a working-class
shopping centre in suburban London. The team
leader was Hughes (USA) which, with Marconi
(UK), Thomson-CSF (France) and Telefunken
(Federal Germany) supplied hundreds of modern
radars for surveillance, heightfinding and
gap-filling. Selenia (Italy) secured the contract for
the hundreds of standardised display and operator

interface consoles. Signaal of the Netherlands was
another powerful contributor. There were many
breakthroughs in devising the all-electronic
computerised control and communication system,
which in seconds can locate and display aircraft
tracks and unambiguously label them as either
friendly or otherwise.

There were also breakthroughs in the matter of
programme management and finance. How does
one allocate costs, when in fact thousands of
companies in 14 countries are involved, but only
nine of those countries are hosts, ie have NADGE
sites on their territory? How does one apportion the
penalties for technical risk or contractual delay? It
was only after prolonged work by contract lawyers
that the precise wording of thousands of clauses was
agreed. Only later was it realised that things could
come unstuck; for example it was written in black
and white that all drawings for the circuit diagrams,
the radar and computer cabinets, the complex
environmental systems, the antennae, the buildings
and the sites, would in all cases be passed within 60
(or sometimes 90) days by the authority of each host
government. But Greece and Turkey, two of the
most important host nations because of their size
and number of sites, are not very well supplied with
electronics engineers, and when many drawings had
been gathering dust for two years the precisely
worded clauses were no help. Even in the basic
funding there were major snags, because while all
partners had agreed the original funding at
£110million, the future rate of inflation had been
predicted at 1¼%! When it went into double figures
the companies began to think of the spectre of
bankruptcy, and after agonising problems a vast
EAP (Equity Adjustment Program) had to be rushed
through to cover the soaring extra costs.

The one really good thing was the programme
itself, which by 1975 had at last given the European
nations a shield, or rather the basis for one. From
that time on, hundreds of Warsaw Pact jets could
thunder over Western Europe at low level, but they
would be detected, and the precise information on
the trajectory, height, speed and future positions of
every target would stream into the NADGE
computers. Without such a system there can be no
defence of Western Europe.

NADGE, however, is far from the end of this
part of the story. NADGE cannot shoot anything
down; that is up to the active defences, as discussed
later. Moreover, since 1975 the system has been
extended and updated, but sadly this has been done
in a more piecemeal fashion. Even the original
system never embraced the UK, which adhered to
the view that, as it already had quite a good defence
system, it did not need another one. Thus, in the
original plan, special interfaces were added to join
NADGE to the old British scheme, parts of which
had hardly changed since World War 2 (as

described in another Ian Allan book, Jack Bushby's *Air Defence of Great Britain*). Subsequently, the British did put in an almost completely new system, called UKADGE. Federal Germany, feeling exposed opposite the world's greatest concentration of military forces, has spent large sums on a complete update of its own air defence system, though as far as possible whilst maintaining compatibility with its neighbours. France's NADGE system was integrated only to the point at which reporting ends and the control of active weapons begins, and has since installed further purely national radars and computer sites. Beyond France, Spain, now a full member of NATO, contracted with Hughes for its own system, originally based on NADGE, called Combat Grande. And, predictably, Norway remains a problem because of its colossal length, and Greece and Turkey remain even greater problems because of their physical size, lack of money and skilled manpower, and political unreliability which in 1975 extended to open warfare between them and withdrawal of the vital Greek stations from the NADGE chain, thus leaving a large gap.

Since 1975 every NADGE host nation has done something to update its air-defence sites and communications. Even in the mid-1970s the latter were still far from perfect. The entire system has always been to some degree vulnerable to sabotage, a fact which has been constantly studied by NATO staffs (and, we may be sure, their opposite numbers in Moscow), and to EW interference either by eavesdropping or even direct interference by jamming or signal distortion. Some of the NADGE sites are linked by landlines, in all cases

Below:
From grass fields in the 1930s, military airfields developed by the mid-1940s into major installations with three tarmac or concrete runways and a surrounding perimeter track from which led taxiways to as many as 130 dispersals, often protected by blast walls. Today airfields are even less mobile and even more vulnerable. These drawings are to the same scale.

independent of ordinary PTT (GPO) telephones, while in all the most important locations microwave links beam the signals between tower-located dishes. The entire network has been operating for 10 years, a long enough period to iron out the initial 'bugs' and achieve high reliability. On the other hand, with the passage of time the entire system becomes both physically tired and technically obsolescent. There have been several important meetings at the highest levels to investigate the prospects for eventually building a new air-defence NADGE 2 using the most modern 1980s technology. The NATO Defence Support Division, which administers both infrastructure and research, in Brussels, has shown how this could be done and what it might cost, but NATO is in that commonest of situations in which the nations, baulking at the astronomic cost, keep deferring a decision until some future year by which time the price will have doubled or quadrupled. Nadgeco has a multinational successor based in Brussels, Eutronic, but this has little 'political clout' and in any case is made up of representatives of aggressive companies (the same as before, as listed earlier) which to a considerable degree are fighting each other for contracts elsewhere. At present there is no sign of a NATO leader with the stature or the money to do anything to break the log-jam, and NADGE plus local add-ons will have to soldier on into the next decade at least.

Of course, NADGE is just the most important of many big NATO infrastructure programmes to provide defence against WP airpower. Another is airfields, though here the underlying trend in many cases appears to be backward. In 1951, when NATO was an embryonic organisation, the situation was a disaster. There were few airfields, and these were of World War 2 layout and location. Thus, until 1957 more than 50% of NATO infrastructure funds were devoted to a gigantic airfield programme. American architects drew a standard BOP (Basic Operating Platform) comprising a single runway of not less than 8,000ft (2,438m) length, plus a large concrete apron and

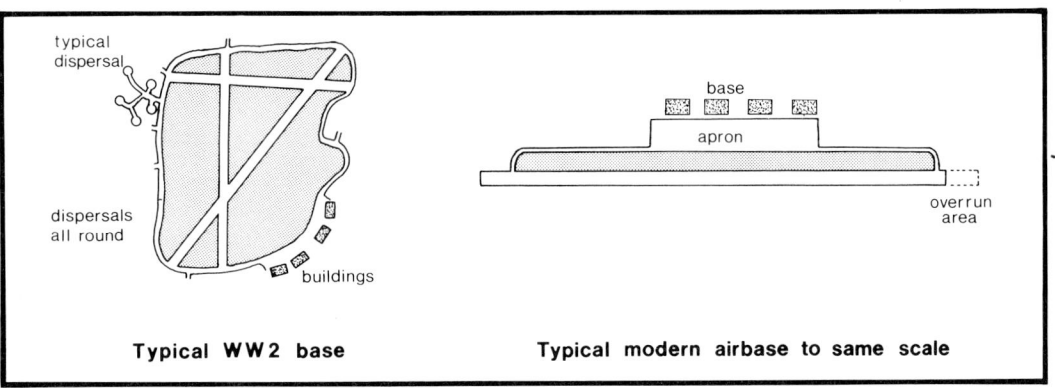

Typical WW2 base   Typical modern airbase to same scale

standardised support buildings, including a US-style control tower packed with American communications. In almost all cases full lighting and ILS were installed, and large storage facilities for Jet A-1 or MIL-F-5616 fuel (in the early years, aviation gasoline as well). After they were built, these new airfields were in some cases extended, and many were fitted with All-American Engineering arrester gear to halt brakeless aircraft without costly barrier crashes or overruns.

In May 1970 NATO's Defence Planning Committee commissioned AD70, or Allied Defence in the Seventies, as a basic fact-finding and policymaking backup for future planning. It noted the rapidly growing capability of WP forces to destroy NATO airbases, using various weapons including uninterceptable missiles, and this led to EDIP (European Defence Improvement Programme) as an initial attempt to do something about it. EDIP was adopted by the Eurogroup, the informal association of the 10 European NATO members at that time, and thus led both to improvements in forces and to additional infrastructure. Of the latter the most important in the context of this book was the HAS (hardened aircraft shelter) programme.

Top:
Most HASs have end closure doors, this British pattern having externally braced doors which slide sideways. The Tornado GR1 comes from RAF No 617 Squadron. It is the intention that all front-line NATO European combat aircraft should have HAS protection, though this seems a very dangerous alternative to widespread dispersal. *BAe*

Right:
Hahn AB was fully provided with HAS protection before it became home to the 50th TFW equipped with F-16 Fighting Falcons. In theory it is possible to use a powered loader to bomb-up the F-16 inside the shelter. *GD*

Far right:
This HAS at RAF Brüggen has a loudspeaker above the number 38 but no visible exterior floodlights. The Jaguar GR1 from No 31 Squadron is being towed in by cables to the main gears, with external steering as shown. *RAF Germany*

Hardened shelters are a natural extension of sandbagged revetments as used in 1940 to offer some protection to tactical aircraft parked at readiness on their bases. They are intended to give complete protection against near misses by conventional weapons, even including bombs of 1,000lb (454kg) size. They also offer virtually complete protection against chemical weapons, but they cannot attempt to withstand nuclear weapons and are also largely irrelevant to biological warfare. As for direct hits by conventional munitions, the protection given obviously depends on the weapon and how it hits. A direct hit by a conventional bomb or rocket with a warhead under 220lb (100kg) might well be fully resisted. A shaped charge or special concrete-piercing (anti-runway) weapon would probably blast a hole and severely damage the aircraft inside the shelter, and even small charges such as those dispensed by the Western Beluga, JP233 or MW-1 tactical aircraft pods might cause a sufficiently violent detonation to spall material off the interior. Conversely an FAE (fuel/air explosive) store going off in the immediate vicinity is capable of generating enough local overpressure to push the shelter sideways or collapse it vertically. So the best one can say is that the HAS programme was far better than nothing. If a hostile air force was so idiotic as to rain down ordinary free-fall HE on a

NATO airbase, the number of parked aircraft seriously damaged might be expected to be about 1%, whereas without HASs the figure might well be 90%. Thus, we can at least be sure the WP generals will never waste time on conventional bombing of NATO airfields.

Each HAS is a steel-reinforced concrete hangar, to one of three standard designs, tailored to accommodate one (in a few cases two) aircraft. One type is arched with circular-arc frames, the others being made up of four to six flat panels with sloping side walls. The ends are closed by doors reminiscent of those of a bank vault, hinged to the shelter and with the weight supported on curved steel tracks. Inside the shelter is strip lighting, electric and pneumatic (and possibly hydraulic) power, and an environmental system giving heating or cooling with anti-NCB filtered air. Of course, the shelters are dispersed over each airfield as widely as possible, though usually located on existing taxiways, so that any single hostile weapon is unlikely seriously to affect more than one shelter. The shelters were the chief element in the ASM (aircraft survival measures) programme, which by the late 1970s had provided such protection for 70% of the aircraft at each base, though at the outset the assumption was that it would be provided for 100%.

It is significant that in the HAS programme there has been no attempt at camouflage, nor any attempt to build cheap dummy shelters over either real or fictitious aircraft. Camouflage, dummies and decoys have been important in air warfare right up to the Yom Kippur war in October 1973, but the consensus of opinion today is that such things are of little value in Central Europe in the 1980s. Back in

World War 2 decoy ground targets were often built close to devastating concentrations of flak, but today there is barely enough funding in NATO to provide adequate protection to the real airbases, and no guns or missiles can be spared to put round decoys.

This is despite a serious decline in the number of active NATO airbases. At the completion of the big infrastructure effort in 1952-59 NATO had 220 operational airfields, but today virtually the whole of NATO's airpower is parked on a mere 63 locations. Indeed, knocking out only 30 airbases would cripple NATO's air strength in Europe (obviously ignoring France, Switzerland, Sweden and Austria) until reinforcements could fly in from the USA, and in the author's view this is an unacceptably small figure. It makes little difference that nearly all the 220 airbases could be readied for use in, say, 72 hours, because a pre-emptive strike would catch the aircraft on the bases where they are now, not at some hypothetical future time. Again, it comes down to a question of money: it is expensive to resurrect disused airfields, even for dispersal or emergency use only.

Though not very exciting, mention should also be made of the NATO Pipeline System. Started in 1953, this is a vast network of large pipes, totalling about 6,300 miles (over 10,000km), as well as storage (often in the pipelines themselves) for over 70,000,000cu ft (1,982,000cu m) of the products handled. At first the products were mainly kerosene grades for jet aircraft and gasolines (petrols) for piston-engined aircraft and land vehicles, these being pumped from Atlantic and Mediterranean ports to airfields and other distribution centres.

Below right:
Improved Hawk is the most important airfield defence SAM in the European NATO nations. This triple launcher belongs to the Royal Netherlands AF

5th Group (Guided Weapons). Total RNethAF strength is 11 squadrons with two triple launchers each. *RNethAF*

Left:
Adorned with the flags of the NATO nations, this was the first Nike Hercules to be completely modified, updated and refurbished in Europe. The inspector here is a McDonnell Douglas engineer, and this was the first of 11 missiles fired at Salto di Quirra test range, Sardinia, in May-July 1981. *McDonnell Douglas*

Below:
NATO's SAMs are nothing like as varied or as numerous as those of the WP forces, neither are they so mobile (except for the very small weapons) nor available in sufficient quantity to fight a war lasting more than a few hours; Bloodhound and Nike Hercules are virtually obsolete. Much depends on Patriot, planned for US Army use from 1970, which after astronomic cost increases is now at last coming into use not only with the US Army but also with some European NATO nations (although Belgium has pleaded insufficient funds to purchase the system).

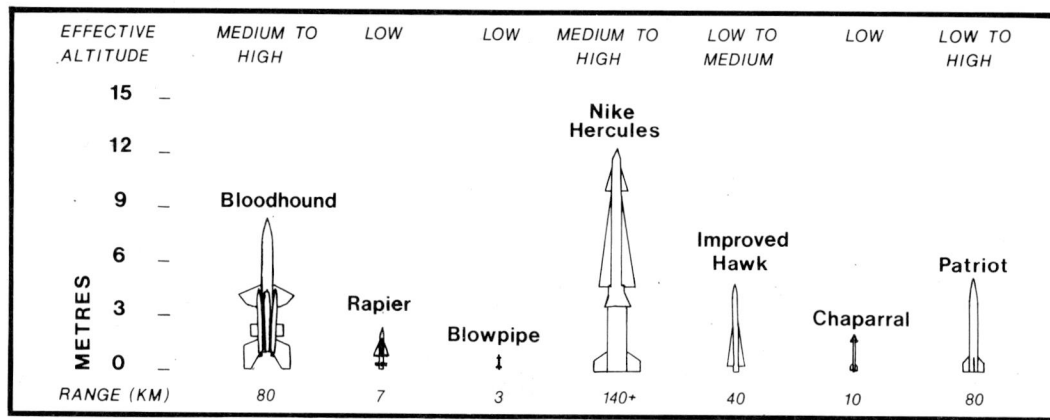

EFFECTIVE ALTITUDE	MEDIUM TO HIGH	LOW	LOW	MEDIUM TO HIGH	LOW TO MEDIUM	LOW	LOW TO HIGH
	Bloodhound	Rapier	Blowpipe	Nike Hercules	Improved Hawk	Chaparral	Patriot
RANGE (KM)	80	7	3	140+	40	10	80

Today gasolines have largely given way to diesel fuels. The main network, of considerable complexity, is in the Central Sector, where over 3,400 miles (5,500km) of large pipe extends through five countries. Other pipes extend from Norway to Turkey.

Protecting such a pipeline system against sabotage is just one of countless tasks calling for a modern system of communications. Telecommunications is almost as big a drain on funds as aircraft and airfields, the total today having exceeded 500 million IAU (a NATO Infrastructure Accounting Unit was originally based on the pound sterling). By the 1970s over 31,000 miles (50,000km) of landlines, radio (microwave) links and submarine cables had been installed to supplement the existing telephone systems in the NATO European nations, but even this was totally inadequate. Should WP forces attack, the system as it was in, say, 1970 was far too slow and too open to interference and breaches of security.

The first major advance in NATO communications was the Aces High tropo-scatter network built in the 1960s to provide high-capacity microwave voice and telegraph circuits from North Cape to Mount Ararat, but covering the whole NATO region rather than the fence-like belt of NADGE. In December 1967 the decision was taken to establish a NATO-wide communications system which, among other things, links all the capitals including Washington and Ottawa. As part of this a NATO Satcom (satellite communications) programme was launched, and the first of two Phase II satellites became operational in March 1970. But, as noted above, more was needed, and in December 1970 it was agreed that the whole NATO C³ (command,

control and communications) within the NATO nations needed to be completely updated, to provide for completely automatic switching and increased-capacity telephone and telegraph channels. The result, which has been coming into use during the early 1980s, is NICS (NATO Integrated Communications System), one part of which is the Phase III Satcom system with far more capable satellites and many extra ground terminals in all NATO countries except France, Luxembourg and Iceland.

Much more continues to be done to improve security of C³ and of stored supplies, and to increase dispersal of all crucial items, if possible to locations unknown to potential enemies. Camouflage is commonly employed to offer what protection it can to such locations, though today it has to be subtle. Multispectral reconnaissance sensors can 'see' much more than the human eye, so that, for example, an item covered with foliage stands out like a sore thumb because of the changed appearance of the cut leaves when viewed at infra-red wavelengths.

Active defence
Fighter aircraft of the NATO air forces are discussed, together with EW/ECM hardware, in the next chapter. This section deals chiefly with NATO's ground-based airfield-defence systems, notably AAA and SAMs. A further vital cog in the machine, AEW/AWACS aircraft, figures in the next two chapters and so is not discussed here.

Older readers will remember the arguments that resulted from the statement, published in the April 1957 British *White Paper on Defence*, that all combat aircraft would soon be replaced by missiles of various kinds. Clearly, missiles could hardly replace manned aircraft in the maritime or surveillance roles, but one area in which elimination of manned aircraft was expected to be almost immediate was air defence. SAM (surface-to-air missile) systems were considered to be far more lethal and cost/effective, and in fact the

advantages of missiles are so great that even today the case is still argued for and against the retention of manned aircraft in the pure interceptor role.

The first SAMs to be deployed on NATO's Central Front in Europe were the Nike Ajax and Hawk of the US Army, Thunderbird 1 of the British Army, Bloodhound 1 of the RAF, and Parca of the Franch army. Soon Nike Ajax was replaced by the extremely powerful Nike Hercules, and this enormous non-mobile weapon system was also deployed by Federal Germany, Belgium, Denmark, Greece, Italy and Norway. Despite its large physical size, its heavy demands for electrical power, manpower and many other services, its immobility (today a graver disadvantage than in the 1950s when the system was new) and its generally poor performance against low-level targets in an environment of sophisticated countermeasures, Hercules is still used by NATO nations and is included in the accompanying table of operational SAMs.

Continued deployment of Nike Hercules results from the extremely long development timescale of Patriot, its planned replacement, which is discussed later. Patriot is also seen as the replacement for Hawk, which for the past 20 years has been the most important NATO SAM system.

HAWK (Homing All-the-Way Killer), more usually written Hawk, was designed in 1954-56 as the US Army's first battlefield mobile SAM. It was planned as a triple launcher on one vehicle, backed up by other vehicles carrying the battery control centre, radars and support systems. The MIM-23A Hawk missile, though smaller and neater than Nike Hercules, was still a hefty weapon with a length of 16ft 10in (5.12m) and firing mass of 1,280lb (580kg). For the first time, CW (continuous wave) radar guidance was used, with semi-active homing on the target, and this was specially designed to provide good enough clutter discrimination to be effective against supersonic targets flying at tree-top height, even in conditions of ECM. The limits of effective target height have always been given as 100ft to 36,000ft (30-11,000m). Hawk soon showed excellent effectiveness and in January 1960, admittedly without any attempt at making life difficult for the SAM, an early production missile destroyed a supersonic Honest John artillery rocket. This was the first time a supersonic target had been destroyed by a supersonic missile.

In January 1958 Hawk was adopted by France, Federal Germany, Belgium, Italy and the Netherlands. These nations formed an industrial consortium called SETEL which shared licence manufacture in proportion to each nation's purchase of complete Hawk weapon systems. By 1967 this phase was completed, with over 4,000 missiles delivered at a cost of over $600million. By this time the US prime contractor had developed Improved

Below:
The RAF Regiment is still responsible for protecting the Sovereign Base Areas on Cyprus, but Bloodhound SAMs have been withdrawn to the UK since this picture was taken. The entire system, however, was designed to be air portable. *MoD (RAF)*

Bottom:
These Lancer Boss sideloaders are among the mass of special ground system equipment forming part of the Bloodhound Mk 2 SAM weapon system. Those in service in the UK are all assigned to dispersed flights of No 85 Squadron, whose hexagon badge has been famous since the days of the SE5a. *MoD (RAF)*

Hawk, with new radars, greater flight performance, a larger warhead and many other updates including the adoption of the 'certified round' technique whereby each Improved Hawk missile is delivered ready to fire without any field maintenance or testing. Accordingly, under the HELIP (Hawk European limited improvement programme) project, the new weapon system was procured by the original team minus Belgium but with the addition of two new customer/participants, Greece and Denmark. Subsequently, in 1979, Belgium placed a $105million order with the US contractor, Raytheon, with about half the work farmed out to European companies, for the Improved Hawk missile.

Previously Spain had been a customer for the US-built Hawk system, so Hawk will continue in widespread use throughout most of the European NATO nations until near the end of the century. Few systems have enjoyed such a long active life.

France soon withdrew Parca, adopting Hawk instead, but today its much more modern, but small short-ranged Crotale mobile SAM system is used to defend Armée de l'Air bases (though these are not part of NATO). In Federal Germany the RAF had for almost 20 years used the British Aerospace Dynamics (previously Bristol/Ferranti) Bloodhound 2 system, which offered great advantages over the Mk 1 in missile flight performance and in its radars, which gave outstanding semi-active homing on to targets down to tree-top height at ranges out to beyond 50 miles (80km). Now redeployed to protect East Anglia airfields, Bloodhound 2 is a powerful missile with proven high lethality against any size of aircraft, the only real drawback being that it is a case of overkill against many tactical aircraft because it was planned to destroy very large long-range bombers. RAF Germany Bloodhounds were deployed in detached flights all administered by No 25 Squadron. Though the system is land mobile and air portable, these flights were essentially on fixed bases at the chief RAF airfields in the Central Sector.

The RAF Regiment also uses a much later SAM, Rapier, and this has also been adopted by the USAF for the defence of its airfields in Britain. Rapier, which gained much favourable publicity during Operation 'Corporate' in the Falklands – where fire

Top:
One advantage of its small size is that Rapier missiles can be easily loaded on the quad launcher by hand – in this case by cadets of the Swiss army. Despite this, the missile is effective out to beyond four miles (6.5km). *BAe*

Left:
The basic guidance of the simplest from of Rapier is optical target tracking and TV missile tracking, with one-man operation. Here a Rapier crew from No 63 Squadron RAF Regiment practise at a German airbase. In the UK three squadrons – in order of forming, Nos 66, 19 and 20 – will protect seven USAF airbases. *MoD (RAF)*

Top left:
The DN181 differential tracking radar gives Rapier a 'Blindfire', day/night all-weather capability. No other SAM system has demonstrated direct hitting capability with radar tracking. *BAe*

Top right:
Tracked Rapier is a self-contained weapon system carried on an FV548 armoured tracked vehicle. It offers full NBC protection and amphibious capability, with eight missile at instant readiness. This vehicle is now serving with the British Army in Germany.

Above:
Latest of the Rapier SAM systems, Laserfire is a self-contained package which fits any convenient-sized truck, and is air-portable beneath medium helicopters. It has four ready-to-fire missiles, plus a surveillance radar and automatic laser tracking to provide day/night clear-weather lethality at low cost. *BAe*

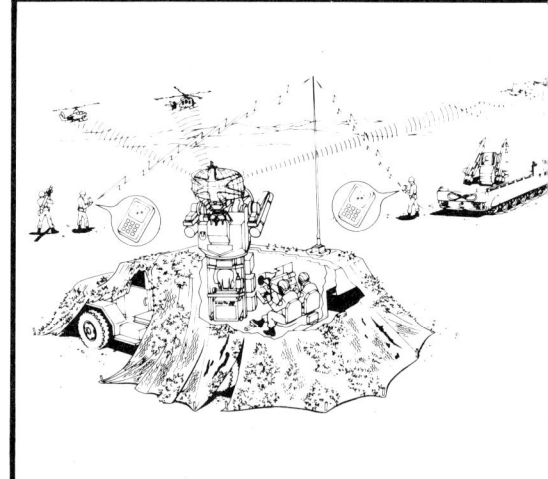

Top left:
Developed by Euromissile, a joint Franco-German company, the Roland SAM has to be deployed aboard substantial vehicles, this SPZ Marder being the choice of the Federal German army. The combined vehicle, which has two missiles ready to fire, is known as the FLaRakPz (anti-aircraft rocket, armoured). The same radar/launcher group is mounted on a large eight-wheel vehicle in the FLaRakRad (AA rocket, wheeled) to be used by the Luftwaffe and Marineflieger for airbase protection. *MBB*

Top right:
Boeing personnel are training US Army instructors and other key personnel on the US Roland fire unit on the XM975 vehicle, but the planned major deployment will not now take place. The programme has been cut back to a single light battalion for the Rapid Deployment Force, with the same fire unit mounted on the M812A1 truck. *Boeing*

Left:
The US Army's Roland air defence system can provide target direction data for other clear-weather short range surface-to-air missiles. Centre, the operator of the planned position indicator in the Roland fire unit (seated to the left of the fire unit commander) selects incoming radar-located targets on the display screen. Position information is then sent via radio to squad leaders of Redeye (left) and Chaparral (right) who have hand-held units which display the location of incoming targets.

Above:
Because of repeated failures of the planned replacements, notably US Roland, the Chaparral system is now expected to remain the US Army's forward area low-level air-defence system until the end of the century! This version mounts the Sidewinder-type missiles on the M730 amphibious vehicle. *Ford Aerospace*

units went straight into action on boggy ground in blizzards after being bumped about on deck for up to three weeks – is a new-technology missile designed to be so accurate that its warhead explodes inside the target aircraft. This concept, known as a 'hittile', enables the physical size of the entire weapon system to be scaled down, with across-the-board advantages in bulk, weight, cost and mobility. RAF Germany has since 1976 used the optical version developed to provide protection against large numbers of hostile aircraft in conditions of good day visibility. Later the Blindfire radar was added to extend the lethality of the system to night and bad weather. The British Army has also adopted the fully mobile Tracked Rapier in which eight ready-fire missiles are carried together with the optical tracker and optional radar on an RC-748 amphibious armoured vehicle. A point worth noting is that the USAF Rapiers, which are likely to be extended to add protection for USAF bases in Federal Germany, are in the UK manned by the RAF Regiment, a novel use of host-nation troops to man the defence at a US facility.

Commercially a rival to Rapier, the Franco-German Roland is not a hittile and thus for the same lethality has to be larger and heavier (launch weight 139lb, 63kg, compared with 99lb, 45kg). The original Roland I, now is service with the French army mounted on AMX-30 tank chassis, is a visual clear-weather weapon only. Roland II adds a monopulse target tracking radar to give a measure of all-weather capability, and this is in service with the Federal German Army and Norway. Roland II was also adopted as the future

standard SHORADS (short-range air defence system) of the US Army, but in a licensed form built by Hughes and Boeing. US Roland consumed large amounts of funding over the long development period from 1974, but finally gave so much trouble it was abandoned as a standard weapon and is used only on a small scale by the RDF (Rapid Deployment Force), which is not normally to be found in Europe. In its place the US Army is continuing to buy the MIM-72C Improved Chaparral, the SAM version of the Sidewinder AAM. Originally an interim replacement for the cancelled Mauler SAM, Chaparral was then a stop-gap to be replaced by Roland, but continues to hold the fort until some better close-range air-defence weapon, such as Tracked Rapier, can be provided. Add-on all-weather capability has been extensively tested, including the British DN181 Blindfire radar used in the Rapier system.

For the future the most important large long-range SAM for many of the NATO countries, including the USA, will be the MIM-104 Patriot. Originally called AADS-70 (Army air-defence system for 1970) it has had one of the longest development periods of any Western weapon system, and despite enormous funding expenditures was still only just beginning to reach the front-line troops in 1983. The missile is large (over 17ft, 5.2m, long), has a nuclear or large conventional warhead, and is usable against targets of all kinds irrespective of numbers, height, speed, weather or countermeasures. A key element in this very costly system is a phased-array radar with electronic scanning able to provide TVM (track via missile) guidance to a salvo of Patriots engaging a number

Left:
Probably the most expensive production SAM in history, the MIM-104 Patriot is a very large system which has been developed for the US Army over the past 22 years, initially as FABMDS, AADS-70 and SAM-D. At last it is entering service, though the price of each fire unit (with missiles) is close to $100million. Here part of a fire unit is on manoeuvres. *Raytheon*

Right:
The Patriot missile is relatively simple, though its guidance uses a sophisticated radar TVM (track-via-missile) method claimed to be 'virtually immune to electronic countermeasures'. The massive missile measures 17ft 5in (5.31m) in length. *Martin Marietta*

Below:
Firing one of the four missile tubes of a Patriot launcher. This important and effective weapon is being deployed by the US Army in Europe. It has also for many years been the subject of discussion by European NATO nations who are supposed to be participating in the programme, but the position is uncertain. Belgium withdrew in 1983 because of shortage of funds. *Raytheon*

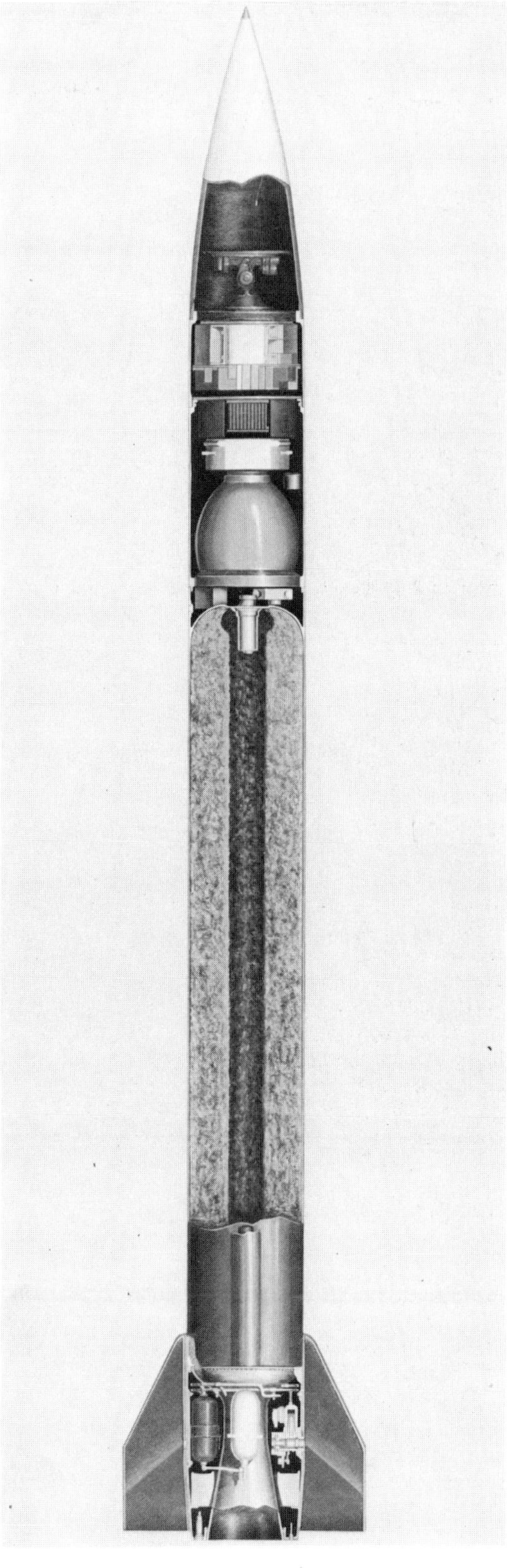

Top left:
FIM-92A Stinger, a vast improvement over Redeye, is now widely deployed as the man-portable air-defence system of the US Army and Marine Corps. It has been used by the Army in West Germany since early 1981. By 1984 the POST (proposed optical Stinger) will be adding 'two-colour' guidance, of the kind long used by corresponding Soviet weapons. *GD Pomona*

Top right:
Redeye is at last being replaced in front-line units with several NATO armies, but it is still around in great numbers. This launcher was being used at Fort Bliss to instruct junior soldiers in how to engage hostile aircraft (no easy job with Redeye). *US Army*

Above:
The simple Blowpipe system was credited with destroying nine hostile aircraft plus two probables in the Falklands, in conditions far removed from those seen here during a demo by the Royal Artillery. This optically tracked radio-command missile is also used by the RAF and Royal Marines, and nine other countries.
British Army of the Rhine

Facing page:
France's SATCP (surface-to-air, very short range) is due to enter service in 1986. It has an IR homing head, and variants are being developed for air-to-air use from front-line helicopters. *Matra*

of individual targets simultaneously. Development funds are still being voted, but the number of missiles to be bought in 1981 to 1984 fiscal years is respectively 130, 176, 376 and 664, so real numbers are at last beginning to appear. The main problem is price, which has yet to get down to $2million for a bare missile. Despite this, six European NATO countries have signed a Memorandum of Understanding to buy Patriot as a replacement for Nike Hercules – which is desperately overdue – and the NATO Patriot Management Office has since 1982 been investigating the possibility of building some or all of this advanced and complex system in Europe.

Though useful only at close range, man-portable SAMs are widely used in NATO, as they are in WP armies. The first, and still very widely used, is the US Army/Marines Redeye, though this has so many shortcomings it is hardly worth the effort of carrying it around. It has no IFF, and thus the user has to find out for himself if the target aircraft is friendly. Moreover, as it homes on the hot jetpipe, it cannot be locked-on to an attacking aircraft but instead must be fired as the aircraft is flying away. US forces call Redeye FIM-43, Federal Germany calls it Fliegerfaust, and Denmark the Hamlet. The far better second-generation Stinger, FIM-92A, can be fired with quite high lethality against any aircraft, even a helicopter or propeller aircraft generating little IR signature, and from any aspect, even head-on. Production in the USA is running at about 4,700 a year, priced at about $80,000 a round, and Federal Germany is negotiating to make production Stingers. There is a related missile used in an air-launched form called ADSM, for air-defence suppression missile, fired from battlefield helicopters. Stinger and ADSM can have dual-wavelength guidance, IR plus UV (ultra-violet).

In the matter of 'Triple-A' (flak) NATO is almost as badly off in comparison with WP forces as in the area of SAM deployment. This is mainly due to the usual problem, shortage of money, but attitudes of mind did not help. Britain thought the SAM would render guns as obsolete as manned fighters, and in this belief the United States to a large degree followed suit. Though retaining guns of 20mm calibre, most notably in the form of the excellent M61A-1 Vulcan which is also used in aircraft and can fire at rates up to 6,000 round/min, the US Army retired all its large AA guns in the 1950s and followed in the early 1960s by scrapping the twin-40mm tracked AA vehicles. What changed everyone's mind was the deadly effectiveness of the widely used Soviet ZSU-23-4 which can go anywhere, is amphibious and fires 23mm shells at rates up to 1,000 rounds/min for each of the four barrels, which are water-cooled for sustained firing with rapid-reload 65-round magazines. In the Yom

Kippur war this ubiquitous flak vehicle devastated the initial Israeli low-level attacks, and overall caused more Israeli aircraft losses than any other single weapon. This could hardly be ignored, and the US Army eventually organised a competition for a new DIVADS (Divisional air defence system) which was finally won by the twin-40mm Bofors made by Ford Aerospace. This fine gun, firing proximity-fused ammunition with high accuracy to ranges of about three miles (4.8km), is carried on a tracked vehicle based on the M48 tank, with all-weather radars for acquisition and tracking, as well as a computer-aided optical system with a laser ranger.

The only Triple-A qualified as a NATO project is Federal Germany's Rheinmetall Rh202 twin 20mm, normally deployed with an analog computing optical sight on a two-wheel trailer – not very different from light flak of World War 2. The same gun is used on various SP vehicles including the Spähpanzer 2 armoured reconnaissance vehicle and the airportable Waffenträger in its AAA version. In these applications the maximum elevation is 60°, which is a common angle in many AFVs. For example, the new 25mm Bushmaster gun fitted to the US Army's Bradley IFV (infantry FV) elevates to 60°. This is considered virtually as good as 90° for engaging attacking aircraft; in fact, more than 90% of the time, hostile aircraft over the battlefield are at an elevation of less than 20° from an observer.

As always, and with most weapon systems, battlefield anti-aircraft weapons are in a state of flux. More than at any previous time, new ideas are overturning established concepts and operating techniques, and some are already on test. One of the possibilities is to deploy missiles that are equally deadly against either AFVs or aircraft. This has never been done, but with IIR (imaging infra-red), laser semi-active homing or millimetre-wave radar homing, all of which are used in current anti-armour weapons, it is unquestionably possible. It is in this kind of advanced guidance technology that the NATO countries hope and believe they still have a slight edge over the WP countries, though the latter's massive development effort must be closing the gap.

NATO's future defences against low-flying aircraft could well include less conventional devices. There are many proposals, some of which are being marketed and demonstrated. One of the ready-for-use schemes is the Rampart system, an integrated array of launchers for smoke, chaff/flare rockets and tethered ballons. A 1983 demonstration by the maker, Wallops Industries of Britain, showed how rapidly a large target area, such as an airfield, can be smothered in smoke, which is first discharged in a rapid-deploy form while a much heavier and more persistent screen is building up. Rocket propelled dispensing cartridges can deploy either IR decoy flares or anti-radar chaff, or (if the nature of the incoming attacker's sensors is not known) both. The Skysnare balloons are Day-Glo orange and are fired to a height of 1,000ft (300m) where they stay, if necessary carrying radar reflectors, to force attacking aircraft up to higher altitude. The only apparent snag is that the defending radar reflectors, chaff and flares just might interfere with friendly SAMs or gun direction systems!

To conclude this chapter, it is worth noting the scale of investment needed in supporting systems to tie together the NATO nations in C^3 (command, control and communications). For many years funding has exceeded \$400million annually purely for electronic installations to update air-defence capabilities, and the rate has had to rise very sharply since 1980. Longest-established system is JTIDS, the Joint Tactical Information Distribution System, into which most tactical aircraft and all AWACS/AEW aircraft are linked. In Europe the dominant communications system has become NICS (NATO integrated communications system), which links satellites and ground stations at all organisational levels down to small tactical units with complete interoperability and improved security. On top of this a major new conceptual programme is MIDS (Multifunctional Information Distribution System) which will use JTIDS technology in CNI (communications/navigation/identification) functions, both in the USA and throughout NATO Europe. Biggest of all is an even newer programme, a really gigantic scheme called ACCS (Air Command and Control System). This will integrate all the offensive and defensive C^3 for all NATO air operations. It will tie together the following systems into one coherent command/control (C^2) structure: NADGE; NAEW (NATO AEW); MIDS; and all offensive C^2 systems.

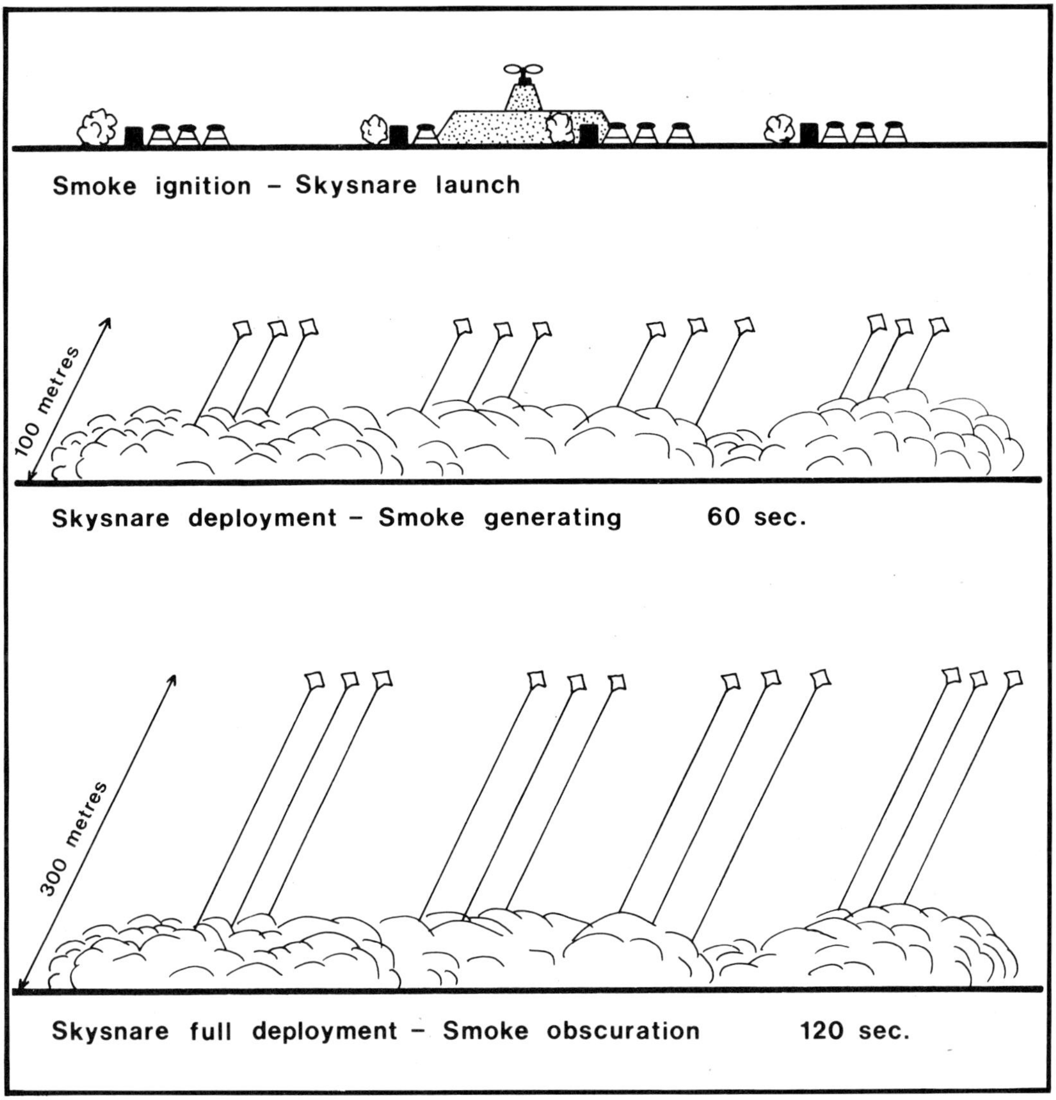

Smoke ignition – Skysnare launch

100 metres

Skysnare deployment – Smoke generating   60 sec.

300 metres

Skysnare full deployment – Smoke obscuration   120 sec.

The NATO Air Defences

Before writing this chapter the author re-read many documents, including relevant chapters of *Brassey's Annual* from 1957 onwards. Many authoritative writers, uniformed and civilian, have spent much time arguing the case for the manned fighter. In Britain, until well into the 1960s, nobody in any official position dared even to do this, or his career would have been in jeopardy. One experienced observer – it would be unfair to name him – went so far as to conclude that, 'The naked truth is, of course, that air defence has become relatively unimportant'.

One has to remember this to put into perspective today's colossal effort to construct defences capable of at least blunting any attack by the WP air forces, and perhaps of either making raids on NATO targets unprofitably costly, or even catching WP aircraft parked on their airfields. Have we all gone mad? All war, of course, is lunacy; but should not NATO's air defences consist of phalanx after phalanx of SAMs, just as the British government appeared to imagine the future would be from a quarter century ago?

In this chapter it is proposed to study the manned fighters, interceptors and tactical attack aircraft of the NATO air forces. It is also important to bring in the use of specialised EW and AWACS type platforms, which will figure importantly in the next chapter which outlines how the NATO ground and air defences might actually operate.

The point has often been made that modern air forces are equipped with many fast jets which might variously be called fighters, or interceptors, or attack aircraft. The demarcation lines have become blurred, and the position is rendered even more confusing by the fact that most of these aircraft can carry external payloads packed with reconnaissance sensors or EW systems such as Elint receivers or barrage ECM jammers. Perhaps the most specialised of the tactical jets is the interceptor, whose mission is to intercept, and if necessary destroy, any other aircraft no matter what the time of day or what the weather. There are not many of these in NATO, though the best by a wide margin will be the Tornado F2 for the RAF. Interceptors are much more common in the WP air forces, where thousands serve with the Soviet PVO-IA (air-defence forces, manned fighters). Interceptors operate from long paved runways well back from the land battle, and they are seldom called upon to do anything except their primary mission.

Of course, any jock who flies an F-14, -15 or -16 would be incensed to hear that he does not fly an interceptor, but in fact these aircraft are best described as fighters, because of their versatility.

Below:

The RAF's Tornado F2 all-weather interceptors have to defend a volume of sky greater than anything previously assigned to a single locally-based force. There is at present no plan to base these aircraft in West Germany (shaded).

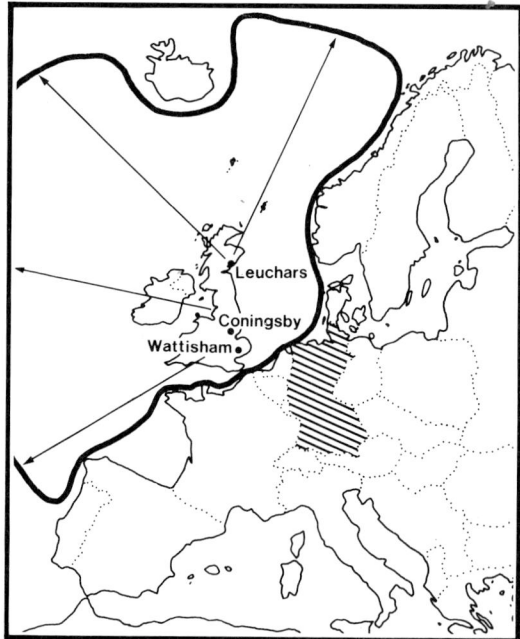

All can carry heavy bombloads, reconnaissance sensors and EW devices tailored to the penetration of hostile airspace. In the same way, the Harrier, Jaguar, Tornado IDS and A-7 all have some air-combat capability; indeed in most US official documents even the A-10 is described loosely as a 'fighter', though it is too limited in flight performance to be very useful against most hostile fixed-wing aircraft. To round off the tactical picture, such machines as the Buccaneer and A-6 have no real air-to-air capability, and on most missions even the fast F-111 lacks the right weapons (though AIM-9 Sidewinders can be carried).

The rest of this chapter is arranged alphabetically, as the most convenient way, without regard to which NATO air force may by the user. Pure attack aircraft are briefly included because of their important counter-air role in attacking WP airbases. The USN/US Marine Corps' A-6 and US marine Corps' A-4 are not included because of the unlikelihood of their participation in any European conflict.

A-7 Corsair 2
Though still important in US Navy embarked Carrier Air Wings, including those with the 6th Fleet, the main European users of the A-7 are the air forces of Greece and Portugal. The former has three *mira* (squadrons) all tasked in anti-ship and other maritime roles, but perfectly capable of effective all-weather land attack using the excellent A-7H, 60 of which were bought new. Portugal obtained 50 A-7Ps, which are refurbished A-7s fitted with updated weapon-delivery avionics. Without a bombload the A-7 is quite agile, can make 600kt (691mph, 1,112km/hr) at low level with low fuel consumption from the unaugmented turbofan engine, and can use gunfire or Sidewinders against other aircraft. The A-7 was (with the F-4) named as recipient for 299 high-power 30mm anti-armour gun pods bought by the USAF in 1981; these are for A-7s of the AFRES (USAF Reserve), which has some 300 of these aircraft in use.

Above:
Vought's A-7 Corsair II proved one of the most cost/effective attack delivery systems ever created, and a few are still in US service, with others in Greece and Portugal. This A-7E came from VA-195, part of CVW-11 aboard USS *Kitty Hawk*. APN

A-10 Thunderbolt II
Unique in concept, in trading flight performance for offensive payload, protection and 'first round' lethality against surface targets, the big and ungainly A-10 has abundantly proved its ability to knock out tanks and other hardened targets when it has the sky to itself, and to survive against small-calibre gunfire. Fairchild Republic delivered 727 to the USAF, including 30 combat-ready two-seat trainers, of which 106 were assigned to the 81st TFW based at two UK airfields, with FOLs (forward operating locations) at four fully manned airbases in Germany. The aircraft was designed around the GAU-8/A gun, the most powerful ever flown (though some slow-firing guns had greater calibre), which can fire milkbottle-size depleted-uranium AP rounds from a giant 1,174-round drum at rates up to 4,200rounds/min. Virtually every NATO air-to-ground store can be carried on 11 pylons, and from 1983 LANTIRN pods were being added to confer much better night/bad weather navigation capability and effectiveness using conventional free-fall bombs, LGBs (laser-guided bombs) and Maverick missiles. Maverick, the most important US tactical ASM, is now in use in its AGM-65D form with IIR (imaging infra-red) guidance for use against armour at night. All-round, the A-10 resembles the Ju 87 Stuka in that unmolested it is devastating; but against WP defences, with eight types of truly modern SAM, attrition would be likely to be catastrophic. The steep dive attacks from over 1,000ft (300m) used in demos of the gun would be suicidal, and the only answer would seem to be to remain 'in the weeds' at the lowest level (where at first many aircraft were lost through hitting the ground during training, though attrition from this cause is now lower).

Top:
Opinions continue to be slightly divided on whether the A-10A Thunderbolt II can really survive over a modern battlefield, though nobody can have doubts about its lethality. Those in USAF Europe are painted in Lizard camouflage, with dark grey insignia, this example at RAF Woodbridge coming from the 510 TFS. *Roger Lindsay*

Above:
Thunderbolt IIs seldom fly as high as this, especially in Europe where survival means going as low as possible without actually flying into the ground. If imitation is the sincerest form of flattery, the Su-25 shows the USAF has got it right.

AGM-109A

Known as 'Cruise' to nuclear protesters, this pilotless aircraft is included because of its importance in the NATO area. At present NATO does not have a single INF (intermediate-range nuclear force) missile, though the Soviet Union has hundreds – over 350 SS-20s alone, each with three individually targeted warheads. It is planned to install 464 AGM-109A Ground-Launched Cruise Missiles at air bases in Britain, Belgium, the Netherlands, West Germany and Italy, each with a single W-80 nuclear warhead. In time of crisis they would leave these bases and disperse (which bombers cannot do). They would free the bombers to concentrate on conventional roles.

Below left:
The fuzziness of this photograph results from the great enlargement from the tracking camera negative. It shows a GD/US Navy Tomahawk cruise missile actually passing through a fabric target on the Tonopah range, Nevada, with an A-7 Corsair II in attendance, in July 1981. Basically the same missile is deployed with the USAF for land tactical use. GD

Below:
The capability of the Tomahawk cruise missile, in all its versions, rests not with any aspect of flight performance (which is not all that different from the V-1 of 1944) but with the amazing guidance system which combines coarse inertial steering with fine-tuning Tercom (terrain contour matching). Here the complete guidance packages are readied for shipment from McDonnell Douglas at St Louis. *McDonnell Douglas*

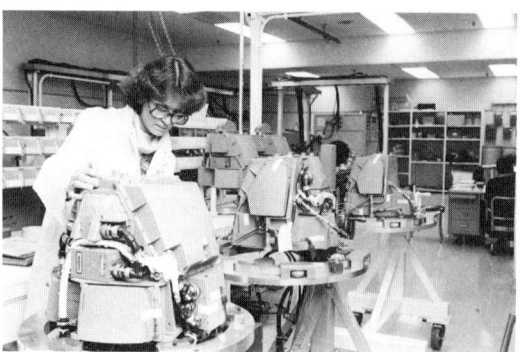

Alpha Jet

Though primarily a trainer, the 175 examples of this Dassault-Breguet/Dornier joint product supplied to the Federal German Luftwaffe are configured for use in the light attack and reconnaissance roles. Of these, the 153 supplied to JaboG 41, 43 and 49 are actually tasked in these roles, the others being attack trainers based in Portugal. They have zero/zero seats, quite good navaids and a Kaiser HUD-sight for the 27mm gun and attack weapons which can include AGM-65A Maverick. Elettronica ECM is fitted, but there is no radar, nor any specialised weapon-delivery system or laser ranger.

AMX

Due to become operational with the AMI (Italian air force) in the second half of 1987, this attack aircraft is a joint programme with Brazil, and uses the Rolls-Royce Spey turbofan engine without afterburner in a form licensed for part-manufacture and assembly to Italian companies. Though subsonic, AMX promises to be an outstandingly cost/effective machine, with the ability to operate with substantial offensive loads from austere unpaved airstrips and fly long missions with great accuracy against any surface target. No search radar is fitted, though one could later be added; this was a decision taken on grounds other than cost and weight. Inertial navigation, advanced cockpit

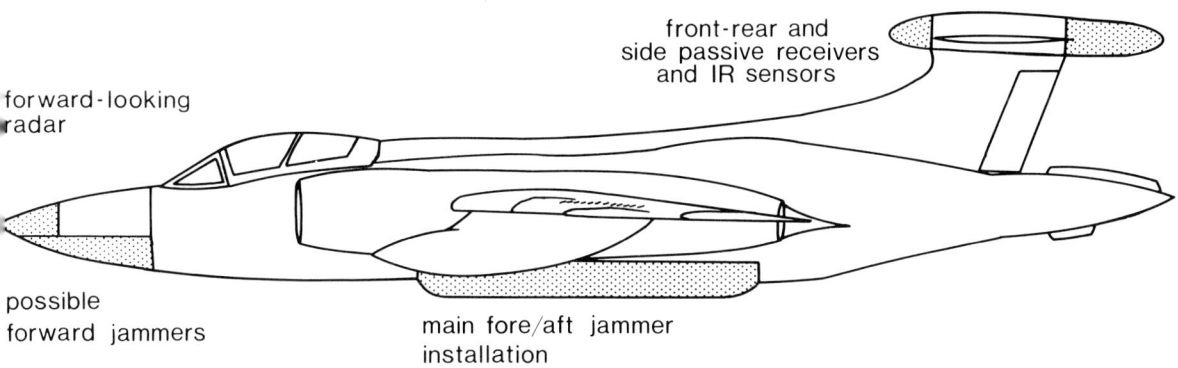

forward-looking radar

front-rear and side passive receivers and IR sensors

possible forward jammers

main fore/aft jammer installation

displays and weapon aiming and the latest EW/ECM suite will be standard in the Italian version, together with an M61 20mm 'Gatling gun'. Italy is buying 187 for close-support, interdiction and reconnaissance, and the air-combat capability of this agile machine should not be dismissed.

Buccaneer

Long derided by the RAF on various ill-founded grounds, this long-range interdictor is so loved by its RAF crews they cannot believe anything can replace it. Tornados are taking over all squadrons except Nos 12 and 216 based in the UK tasked with maritime attack, using the new Sea Eagle missiles among other stores. If this were a Soviet aircraft those withdrawn from use would promptly be rebuilt as ECM platforms, a category of aircraft missing from the British order of battle.

Draken

The Saab 35 Draken may be long in the tooth, but as an all-round combat aircraft it is still extremely effective. The KDF (Royal Danish air force) uses a multirole version in F-35 single-seat and TF-35 two-seat forms, equipping the Karup wing and tasked in attack and reconnaissance roles. They have no major shortcomings, with advanced HUDs and weapon-delivery systems, outstanding STOL rough-field capability and tremendous agility in the air combat role using two 30mm guns and Sidewinders. The KDF has used its F-16s to replace F-100s and F-104s, but not these popular Swedish machines.

Above:
Scorned for over a decade, the Buccaneer finally proved so useful to the RAF that its crews resist being re-equipped – even with the Tornado! This group from XV (No 15) Squadron at RAF Laarbruch will be a sight from the past soon after this book appears, though 'the Bucc' will go on for another 18 months in the maritime strike role. *RAFG*

Bottom left:
Denmark's Swedish-built Drakens are so good they are being kept in service alongside the F-16 (while Sweden itself is having to shut down three Draken squadrons from lack of funds). Here Sqn Ldr John Broadbent from RAF Germany boards a TF-35XD two-seater at Jever, while in the rear is an RF-35XD reconnaissance version. *RAFG*

Below:
Even the TF-16B does not find it too easy to fly rings round the TF-35XD tandem-seat trainer Draken of the Flyvevabnet (RDAF in NATO parlance). Note the low-voltage formation lights showing as bright strips. *Saab-Scania*

Above right:
Departing from Jever, West Germany, after a NATO meet, this Danish RF-35XD is normally based at Karup with 729 Esk (squadron). Among its equipment fits is the Red Baron multisensor pod. *RAFG*

Bottom right:
When first developed in the early 1960s, for the USAF, the reconnaissance version of the F-4 Phantom set a completely new standard in tactical reconnaissance systems and capability. This RF-4C is one of the last USAF F-4s to remain in Britain, with the 1st TRS at RAF Alconbury. *USAFE*

E-3 Sentry

Based on the Boeing 707-320C airframe, this AWACS type aircraft is even today still the most capable in service in the West, and probably in the world, though in many respects it is surpassed by the more modern RAF Nimrod. A particular shortcoming is the location of the giant rotating antenna 'Rotodome' above the fuselage, where its vision is less than perfect and it not only vibrates but has to tilt in any banked turn. Nevertheless the all-round capability of the Westinghouse APY-1 radar is still tremendous, and from the 22nd aircraft delivered to the USAF a maritime surveillance mode is added for use over sea areas. From the 25th aircraft the designation is changed to E-3C, in which the original 13 different radio communications links are replaced by JTIDS, which is a most important system not only for all US forces but also for NATO. JTIDS can link 98,000 users all over the world in a single channel which provides virtually complete security and resistance to jamming or any other interference. This enables a single Sentry cruising at 29,000ft (8,850m) for periods lasting from 6 to 10 hours – a time which can be extended by boom-type inflight refuelling – to study everything in the sky within a radius of 230 miles (370km) for low-flying targets, and to greater distances at high altitudes, and provide complete information for the control of every friendly aircraft. It can offer guidance to interceptors or attack aircraft, allocate the entire friendly order of battle, knowing the status of every item, and its precise location, and provide so much information or precision control as to multiply the effectiveness of the friendly airpower by about three times (an official estimate). USAF E-3As and improved E-3Cs, as well as E-3Bs (As modified close to C standard), may be found in Europe flying with Tactical Air Command. NATO also has a multinational force of 18 Sentries, completed by Dornier approximately to E-3C standard but still designated E-3A, based at Geilenkirchen in Germany or detached elsewhere on the NATO front as needed, manned by crews from several NATO air forces. The one unresolved question is how they can be protected against the extremely sophisticated WP SAM systems, which on paper should be able to destroy such aircraft with ease.

E-6A

The US Navy will deploy 15 of these CFM56-powered aircraft from late 1986, and some will probably be based in Europe. Based on ex-airline 707s, they will replace EC-130Qs in the Tacamo mission as high-flying communications/control (C^2) platforms, some of their duties being to link with E-3 Sentries (and almost certainly Nimrods) and also with distant missile submarines.

F-4 Phantom II

With over 400 of various types still in front-line service in Europe, this is still one of the most important NATO aircraft, being exceeded in numbers only by the Tornado and F-16. One of its great strengths has always been its ability to fly both attack and fighter missions; it has for 25 years been

Right:
Lancaster crews, especially from No 617 Squadron, will need no telling just where this RAF Phantom FGR2 (from No 17 Squadron) was when it was photographed returning to Brüggen from a NATO meet at Baden Söllingen. (The Mohne dam was, of course, rebuilt after the war.) *RAFG*

Below right:
Phantoms are still soldiering on as the UK air defence fighter, and the type will be seen for several years yet. These, carrying twin Sidewinder rails, were with No 29 Squadron, whose personnel provided the original crews for Phantoms defending the Falklands from 1982. *MoD*

Below:
American efforts to bolster the thinly spread and financially constrained Turkish forces are at the same time viewed with suspicion by Greece. In March 1984 the US Congress announced it had been notified by the Pentagon of a plan to sell Turkey a further 15 ex-USAF F-4Es, to augment 82 already serving with four THK squadrons of which this is one. *MCAIR*

Bottom:
From a distance it is not easy to see that this is an F-4G, the Advanced Wild Weasel dedicated EW version of the Phantom, costing approximately four times as much as early F-4 fighter versions. Serving with the 52nd TFW at Spangdahlem, West Germany, these elaborately equipped Elint/ECM platforms also carry weapons and would play a crucial part in any European conflict.

the outstanding example of a 'dual-capable' aircraft. USAFE was for many years the chief European user, with just over 400 at one time, but this total is falling as newer types replace it. User units in 1983 included the 52nd TFW at Spangdahlem (F-4E and the dedicated EW variant, the F-4G); 86th TFW at Ramstein (F-4E); and 406th TFTW at Zaragoza, Spain (various models). The unarmed RF-4C multisensor reconnaissance version equips the 10th TRW at RAF Alconbury and the 26th TRW at Zweibrücken. The German Luftwaffe received 175 F-4Fs, which equip JG71 at Wittmundhafen and JG74 at Neuburg, and JaboG 35 at Pferdsfeld and JaboG 36 at Rheine-Hopsten. The JGs are fighter wings, the others being fighter-bomber units tasked primarily for attack. Interception capability of all F-4Fs will be tremendously enhanced when they are modified with a new multimode radar matched to the AIM-120A AMRAAM missile, as now coming into pilot production for the USAF, USN, USMC, RAF and Luftwaffe. This 'fire and forget' radar-homing missile is by far the best medium-range weapon known, because at last it eliminates the need for the launching fighter to keep flying towards the enemy whilst illuminating it with its radar (as is necessary with AIM-7 Sparrow). AIM-120 flies on inertial guidance until close to the enemy, when it activates its own miniature guidance radar. It figures prominently in future plans for the F-15 and Tornado F2. The Luftwaffe also uses an uprated reconnaissance model, the RF-4E, which is being modified to enable it to fly a limited range of attack missions. Spain has two squadrons of C-12s (F-4Cs) used in the fighter role, Greece has three squadrons of the excellent F-4E (the newest fighter version) and Turkey four squadrons of the same variant tasked mainly in attack missions. The RAF has two squadrons, Nos 19 and 92, based in Germany at Wildenrath, equipped with the fan-engined Phantom FGR2 which has more power than other models but a slower top speed. Other squadrons are based in Britain, but from 1985 will be replaced by the Tornado F2. RAF Phantoms can fire the British Sky Flash missile, which though not

the same generation as AIM-120 is a great improvement in electronic performance and lethality over most versions of Sparrow. It should also be mentioned that, having previously produced the old AIM-9B Sidewinder missile, NATO European nations led by Germany's BGT (Bodenseewerke Gerätetechnik) are now in full production with the far superior AIM-9L version, with all-aspect engagement capability and a better motor and warhead. Early AIM-9Ls were highly effective fired from Sea Harriers during Operation 'Corporate' in 1982.

F-5

Northrop's commercially successful light fighter is used in two generations by NATO forces in Europe. The modern F-5E Tiger II is an important mount for DACT (dissimilar air-combat training) by the USAF 527th 'Aggressors' TFW at RAF Alconbury, which, though a training unit used to hone the skills of already combat-ready fighter pilots, would in emergency play an air-combat role. The earlier F-5A is used by the Netherlands, Norway, Spain, Greece and Turkey, and has recently been withdrawn by Canada. Both single-seat and dual versions are used, with various differences between air forces (for example the Norwegian aircraft, now mainly replaced by F-16s, have assisted-take-off rockets and airfield arrester hooks). All F-5s can fly fighter or light attack missions, and Spain and Turkey use the camera-equipped RF-5 as well. In

clear-weather daytime conditions they are quite fair dogfighters, using Sidewinders and a pair of the single-barrel M39 cannon.

F-14 Tomcat

Standard interceptor of the US Navy, this swing-wing machine is far from new, underpowered and has had extremely prolonged difficulties with its engines, but it still has interception capabilities no other aircraft in the world can match. Its AWG-9 radar can lock-on to one aircraft in a close formation at well over 100 miles' range, or guide missiles on simultaneous attacks on six different aircraft selected from a formation of 24! Another unrivalled capability is the selection of any of four types of air-to-air weapons, which in ascending order of range are a 20mm M61 gun, the AIM-9 Sidewinder, AIM-7 Sparrow (later, AIM-120A) and AIM-54 Phoenix. F-14s can carry a heavy attack load, though they very seldom do, and many have been equipped with the externally mounted TARPS (tactical air reconnaissance pod system), but the primary missions are all standard forms of CAP (combat air patrol) including the escort of friendly attack aircraft. F-14s operate from USN carriers which may be found off many parts of Europe. Post-1986 production will be of the vastly improved F-14D with the F110 engine.

F-15 Eagle

First flown in 1972, this very large and powerful aircraft has ever since been one of the world's top fighters. Indeed it was said in the early days of the (supposedly competing) lightweight fighter programme, 'The only way a lieutenant can make it to captain is by swearing total allegiance to the F-15'. It was planned as the USAF's answer to the MiG-25, but in fact the two aircraft are in no way comparable for the F-15 is a close-combat dogfighter and also a most versatile machine able to carry reconnaissance sensors or a very heavy load of air-to-ground weapons. Apart from tremendous

Top:
Subtly different in outline from the F-5A, the F-5E Tiger II is not used by any NATO country except the USA itself, where the USAF and Navy both picked the type to act the part of WP enemies in air-combat training. But in any European general conflict it would be impossible for Switzerland's four 18-aircraft squadrons not to be involved. *Northrop*

Above:
With interception capabilities so far unequalled by any other aircraft, the F-14A Tomcat is now at last to get a new engine, the F-14D due to enter service in the late 1980s powered by the outstanding General Electric F110. On 19 August 1981 two F-14As of squadron VF-41 became the only modern US interceptors to fire in anger (off the coast of Libya).

Above right:
Bitburg AB is naturally fully equipped with HASs, but these F-15A Eagles of the 36th TFW are parked in the open. This wing, with a nominal strength of 72 but actually possessing about 80 aircraft, is unquestionably the most effective single unit in NATO in providing air defence. But if the Kremlin should ever decide to move west, Bitburg would certainly be wiped off the map before the situation was recognised. *Gordon Bain*

all-round flight performance, the F-15's main advantage over all contemporary aircraft has been its excellent APG-63 radar and advanced displays which are computer-processed to present only the information important to the pilot. It makes air combat almost easy, using an M61 gun, AIM-9 Sidewinders or AIM-7 Sparrow (later AIM-120) missiles. All F-15s have very long range and endurance, extended by boom-type inflight refuelling, and the current production F-15C has provision for Fast packs, which are conformal pallets on the sides of the fuselage which add a further 9,750lb (4,422kg) of fuel with no extra drag and without occupying pylons; indeed the packs add tangential pylons for extra weapons. The F-15C

also introduced a programmable signal processor and many other avionic updates. The USAF bought 729 Eagles and then continued procurement, as well as further development for new capabilities, taking the total by fiscal year 1987 up to a planned 1,107. Among the wings equipped are the 36th TFW at Bitburg, Germany, and the USAF also assigned one squadron, the 32nd TFS, to Camp Amsterdam, Soesterberg, to plug a gap left by the absence in the early 1970s of an all-weather interceptor unit from the Netherlands. The F-15 also equips the US Rapid Deployment Force.

F-16 Fighting Falcon

With almost 500 aircraft, this superb multirole fighter is at present the most important single type in the NATO European air forces. It is built by a five-nation consortium led by General Dynamics of the USA and including companies in Belgium, Denmark, the Netherlands and Norway, with assembly lines in Texas, in Belgium and in the Netherlands. The F-16A and two-seat F-16B have now been followed in production by the first major phase of a staged improvement programme resulting in the F-16C and two-seat F-16D, with further augmented multirole capability for bad-weather and night precision attack and BVR (beyond visual range) interception. In the latter role the weapon will be the AIM-120A (AMRAAM). At present the F-16A is armed in the air-to-air mission with a 20mm M61 six-barrel gun and AIM-9J or -9L Sidewinder close-range missiles. Radar-guided Sparrow and Sky Flash missiles have been fired, but these cannot be guided by the original Westinghouse APG-66 radar. In close air combat no aircraft in the West can stay with a well-flown F-16, which in theory can sustain a 9g turn over most of the flight envelope and is even cleared to 5.5g with heavy bombloads. Users in Europe are: the USAF 50th TFW at Hahn AB, Germany, and 401st TFW at Torrejon, Spain; the FAB (Belgian air force) Nos 349 and 350 Squadrons at Beauvechain and Nos 23 and 31 Squadrons at Kleine Brogel, with four Mirage squadrons (Nos 1,2,8 and 42) at Florennes and Bierset converting; Denmark's Esk 727 and 730 at Skrydstrup; the Netherlands Nos 322 and 323 Squadrons at

Left:
Almost a decade ago the USAF hit on the idea of a 'Hi-Lo mix' of fighters, which had nothing to do with altitude but merely meant that the F-15 (originally sacrosanct) and F-16 (originally a scorned lightweight) could serve alongside each other. It was not then appreciated how good the F-16 would prove to be. Both use Pratt and Whitney's F100 engine, but this monopoly has now been broken in new versions.

Above:
On patrol from Leeuwarden, four
European-assembled F-16As from the KLu's No 323
Squadron get their pilots' bonedomes exactly in
line. The AIM-9J Sidewinders were US-supplied, but
the more advanced AIM-9L is now in collaborative
production in Europe. Close inspection shows that
all three squadron badges (an archer) are peeling off.
Dutch MoD

Below:
An extremely valuable bit of added NATO muscle
was provided by the deployment of the USAF 50th
TFW, equipped with the F-16A and B, to Hahn AB in
1982. It was said that the emphasis would shift from
strike and close support (in the days when the 50th
flew the F-4) to air superiority, but in fact the F-16
has also dramatically enhanced the wing's attack
capability.

Above :

This European-assembled F-16B was on pre-flight walkaround before a mission at the 1982 NATO

Tiger Meet, held at RAF Gütersloh. It flies with the 31st Squadron of the FAB (Belgian AF), based at Kleine Brogel. *Waltermann*

Above :

Just as the KNL (RNorAF to NATO) specified arrester hooks for its F-5s, so has it specified braking parachutes for its F-16s, resulting in the extended section below the rudder. Similar extensions may later become common as a result of the installation (in F-16s of other air forces) of Rapport and similar ECM protection. This F-16A, visiting Soesterberg, comes from 332 Squadron at Rygge.
M. Horseman

Left:

An F-16B of the Flyvevabnet (RDAF) 727 Esk (squadron), from Skrydstrup. Denmark is largely islands, with Copenhagen in the extreme east on the coast facing Sweden. In a recent poll Denmark scored very low in 'Do you believe your forces can defend your country?' but near the top in 'Are you willing to defend your country should war break out?' *GD*

Leeuwarden, Nos 311 and 312 Squadrons at Volkel and (with ex-RF-104G reconnaissance pods) No 306 Squadron, also at Volkel, with several more to convert; and the Norwegian Nos 331 and 334 Squadrons at Bodo and No 332 at Rygge. The USAF and General Dynamics continue aggressively to develop the F-16, on the one hand with a totally CCV (control-configured vehicle) demonstration aircraft able to make lightning-fast manoeuvres in any direction which offers a revolutionary new capability in all forms of air combat and air/ground weapons delivery, and in another programme with the greatly enlarged F-16XL with a cranked-arrow wing which offers either twice the weapon load or dramatically reduced field length and 50% greater radius of action! The latter has since early 1983 been competitively evaluated against the F-15E Enhanced Eagle to select a next-generation all-weather multirole fighter/attack aircraft. The F-15E was chosen, but F-16XL development continues, and the basic F-16 from 1985 will have the new GE F110 engine.

Left:
Though it is impossible to make one aeroplane correctly designed for both air combat and surface attack, especially with a non-pivoted wing, the F/A-18A shows by its official designation that it does both jobs. This mix of Fs and two-seat TFs typifies the Hornets that are replacing A-7s and F-4s in Carrier Air Wings. *MCAIR*

Inset:
In the air combat configuration the F/A-18A carries two medium-range Sparrows and two close-range Sidewinders, though it may eventually be possible to augment this. The Canadian Armed Forces, like all other land-based customers, have accepted the shipboard features of the original aircraft. Note the false canopy painted on the underside. *MCAIR*

Top:
In the clean configuration the Hornet can work up to Mach 1.8, which is as fast as most air forces want to go. In the attack role the long-span fixed wing and external ordnance would hold speed to half this value, though again this is typical of the latest practice. *MCAIR*

Above:
The only Hornets likely to be landbased in Europe are the CF-18s of the Canadian Armed Forces, replacing the CF-104G in the Air Group in Europe, and the 72 (or 84) to be delivered to Spain's EdA from 1986. This is a CF-18B two-seater, in the CAP configuration. CF-18s join No 349 Squadron at Baden-Söllingen in June 1985. *MCAIR*

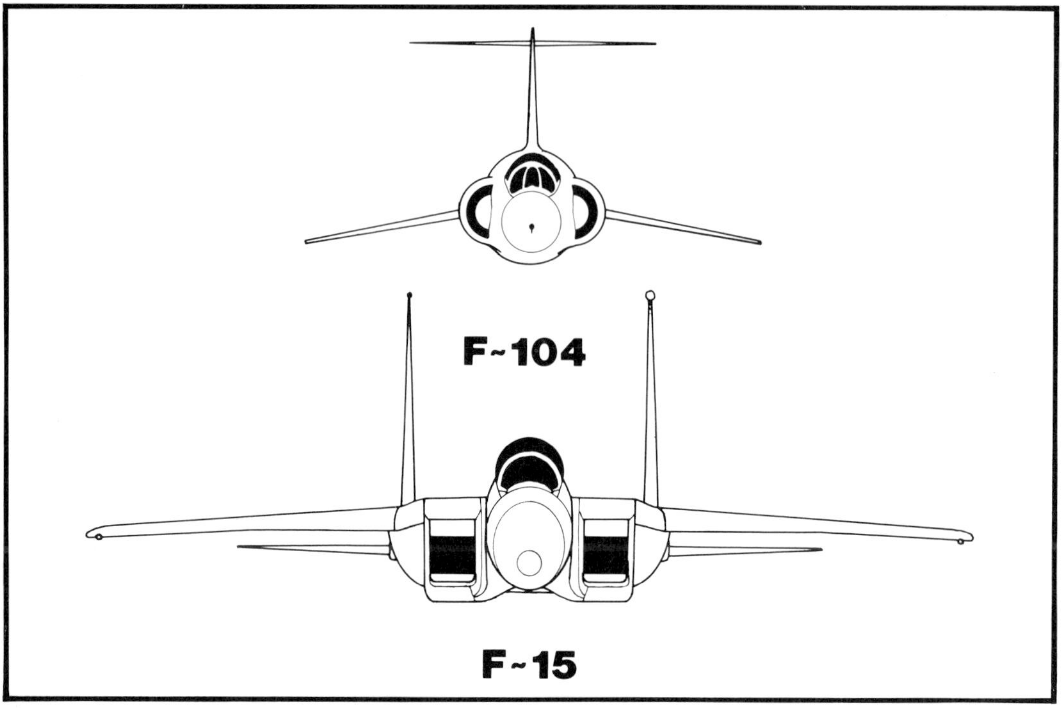

F~104

F~15

Left:
Unquestionably the one area where the F/A-18A Hornet scores over all combat aircraft that preceded it is in its cockpit, which is probably the most carefully optimised that can be attained with contemporary technology. Dial instruments are notably absent, and the scene is dominated by three giant MFDs (multifunction displays) which at a touch can be programmed to call up what the pilot wishes to know. (This is a pilot training simulator.)
Hughes Aircraft

F/A-18 Hornet
Planned as a low-cost replacement for the US Navy and Marine Corps F-4 fighters and A-7 attack aircraft, with the additional possibility of replacing the costly F-14, this matured as an extremely important and capable multirole aircraft which unfortunately happens to be much more costly even than the F-14! Despite this, and failing to meet the numerical mission requirements, the F/A-18 is an outstanding aircraft with near-total multirole capability without changing the avionics, displays, pylons or software. It is tragic that this first-class and extremely valuable aircraft should be rivalling the F-111 in becoming not only the butt of narrowminded critics who cannot see beyond a supposed list of deficiencies, but also a football tossed around in a surely unwarranted dispute between the manufacturing partners, all of which is likely to lead to a reduction in the Navy/Marines buy below the planned 1,366. Hornets will be seen aboard 6th Fleet carriers, and with No 1 Canadian

An inevitable weakness of big fighters, such as the F-14, F-15 and MiG-25/31, is that they can be detected on radar at great distances unless they were designed with stealth technology. Here an F-15 with FAST packs is compared with an F-104G.

Air Group at Baden-Söllingen, Germany, replacing the CF-104G. They have no major shortcomings, either in all-weather attack or in defence using radar-guided Sparrows and later AIM-120s.

F-20A Tigershark
Northrop had not succeeded in finding the vital start-up buyer for this outstanding multirole fighter as this was written in autumn 1984.

F-104 Starfighter
Until 1975 there were some 1,300 Starfighters at readiness in Europe, but by 1984 this number had been reduced to below 350. In the 1960s the type was notorious for the high incidence of pilot fatalities in the Federal German Luftwaffe, but when accurately flown, as in Norway and the Netherlands at the time, its attrition was in no way disquieting. Good features were tremendous flight performance (tempered by poor manoeuvrability) and extremely high penetrative capability with a tiny frontal cross-section, minimal radar reflectivity, very high speed at low level, good all-weather or night navigation, and near-absence of

engine smoke. Versions were produced for ground attack, anti-ship missile attack and multisensor reconnaissance, but the chief surviving model is the Italian-built F-104S all-weather interceptor armed with a 20mm M61 gun, Sidewinders and either Sparrow or Aspide radar-guided missiles. This version equips three AMI *gruppi* in the interceptor role plus a further seven *gruppi* tasked in the strike mission. Turkey has two squadrons flying the same variant, plus two further units equipped with second-hand F-104G attack aircraft. Greece likewise has two squadrons of F-104Gs, based at Araxos in the strike role, but the other once-big users have re-equipped with the F-16 and Tornado.

F-111
Popularly called the Aardvark because of its long nose, and also used in the EF-111A version officially named Raven but almost universally called Electric Fox from its designation, the swing-wing One-Eleven was in its youth the world's most controversial aircraft in history. Critics said it was technically a flop, too expensive, built by the wrong company and ineffective in combat missions in Vietnam. Nothing could have been further from the truth, and in these long-range interdiction aircraft NATO has the capability to strike at any fixed or moving point target within 500 miles (800km) of the Iron Curtain, at night or in the worst weather, with extremely high probability that the target will be hit. It is hard to think of any other

Above:
The F-104G was selected by West Germany in 1959 because of its ability to penetrate hostile airspace at low level, using inertial navigation and carrying nuclear weapons or cameras. It still has this ability, but few are left in Western Europe. This Belgian example will have become Turkish before this book appears. *F. Martin*

Left:
One of the operational advantages of the F-104 has always been its small radar cross-section, which combined with its exceptionally high speed at sea level gives it high penetrability. This Luftwaffe RTF-104G continues to serve in the ECM and operational training role. *BdV (German MoD)*

aircraft that can do this; the Mirage IVA is not a NATO aircraft, the Buccaneer can fly nearly as far but lacks speed and comparable EW systems, and the Tornado has less internal fuel (though smaller and more efficient engines). Suffice to say that the two USAF wings equipped with these swing-wingers are absolutely vital to NATO's offensive capability, and the fact that the One-Eleven, despite its designation, is not a fighter is immaterial. The units concerned are the 20th TFW, flying the F-111E from Upper Heyford, and the 48th TFW flying the more powerful and avionically improved F-111F from Lakenheath (or from Sculthorpe in 1983 while its base runways were being resurfaced). In 1981 the 48th became one of the first units to begin to receive the large Pave Tack pod, carried semi-recessed into the weapon bay, which adds a FLIR (forward-looking infra-red) and laser designator, boresighted together for even greater precision in night or bad-weather delivery. Until the arrival of the Tornado the F-111 was the only NATO aircraft capable of making blind first-pass attacks on point targets, in other words of going at Mach 0.9 direct to a small target and dropping a bomb on it, using its own self-contained navigation systems and weapon-aiming avionics. As well as Pave Tack its attack capability has been enhanced by the addition of new precision missiles such as AGM-65A Maverick and the large GBU-15 cruciform-winged weapon. In addition the F-111 has been evaluated as a carrier for the Pave Mover surveillance and designation radar, in two dissimilar forms made by different companies, to see what advantages this can give in detecting and pinpointing battlefield targets and directing attack aircraft on to them. Pave Mover can also direct guided submunitions fired in surface missiles, the main 'bus' vehicle merely hurling a cloud of small bomblets towards the enemy and the Pave Mover then taking over and making each weapon home to an enemy tank or other target.

There is also a completely different F-111, the unarmed EF-111A, which is already playing a crucial role in providing sophisticated high-power EW detection, control and jamming. This specialised aircraft, deployed in Europe first alongside the 20th TFW, greatly magnifies the effectiveness and survivability of all other NATO front-line aircraft, as explained in the next chapter.

Harrier
Under this heading all Harrier variants are discussed, including the AV-8A, AV-8B Harrier II and Sea Harrier. The original Harrier entered RAF service in early 1969, and soon proved to have unique capabilities. Many critics pretended to see only the so-called 'penalties' of STOVL (short takeoff, vertical landing) capability, among which with 1960s technology were subsonic speed and relatively small payload/range for the available engine thrust. Today understanding is a little better. It is recognised that, in any actual European war, the first thing the NATO air forces would hear would be the sound of conventional – or, more

Left:
Being marshalled ahead on the apron at RAF Lakenheath, this F-111 represents the relatively miniscule NATO force of long-range interdiction aircraft, which face at least eight times as many similar aircraft in the Soviet FA (Frontal Aviation) alone. It was to ease pressure on the overworked F-111s that the BGM-109 was fielded to take over the nuclear attack role, whilst at the same time removing the retaliatory problem of operating from a fixed base. *USAF 48th TFW*

Below left:
When the F-111 was designed it was expected the internal bay would carry either a nuclear bomb or a 20mm M61 gun. In practice, it houses either an extra fuel tank or, as seen here, the big Pave Tack all-weather attack sensor. Pave Tack combines a FLIR (forward-looking infra red) and target designator laser in a single steerable turret.

Below:
The Harrier GR3 normally flies at extremely low altitude on close-support and reconnaissance missions. Until the Falklands campaign it had only simple weapons such as rockets, GP bombs and two 30mm guns. This machine of No 3 Squadron operated from Wildenrath (today Gütersloh); the Phantom is from No 19 Squadron. *RAFG*

Bottom:
Not yet integrated into the NATO command structure, Spain's armoury includes a squadron (Esc 008 of the Arma Aerea de la Armada) of AV-8A Harriers, one of which is seen here in the hovering mode. From 1987 a second unit will form equipped with Harrier IIs. *McDonnell Douglas*

probably, nuclear – explosions on their airfields. Anything on those airfields would be extremely unlikely to survive as far as the start of Day 1. The only way to escape would be to be somewhere else, and STOVL capability is the only known way to accomplish this, by dispersing to any of many hundreds of prepared small strips, preferably terminating in a 'ski jump' slope to multiply the weapon load for a given radius of action. A further advantage of the unique Pegasus vectored-thrust turbofan engine is that not only does it confer outstanding acceleration (because thrust has to be roughly similar to laden weight) but it also enables in-flight manoeuvres to be done which no conventional aircraft can emulate. It was largely the US Marine Corps which discovered the technique of Viffing (VIFF = vectoring in forward flight) with which a Harrier can suddenly zip upwards without changing its attitude, or suddenly appear to stop and fly backwards. This, combined with its physically small size, smokeless engine and strange silhouette, makes it a most agile and slippery air-combat opponent. The RAF Harrier GR3 is configured for ground attack and reconnaissance, rather than air combat, though when well flown its two 30mm guns and up to two pairs of Sidewinders can make it formidable in the latter role also. In contrast, the Royal Navy Sea Harrier was from the start tailored to the air superiority role, with multimode radar, and in Operation 'Corporate' had no trouble disposing of all the high-speed hostile aircraft against which it was directed, notwithstanding often appalling weather. During this campaign many new weapon fits were hastily added, including AIM-9B and -9L Sidewinders on new twin launchers, Paveway smart bombs (laser-guided LGBs), RN 2in rocket pods on RAF Harriers instead of 68mm SNEB pods, new 190gal

Left:
A Harrier GR3 of RAF No 4 Squadron, whose home base is Gütersloh, making a rolling take-off from a public highway in the German countryside. RAF Germany has located numerous sites which, in emergency, might be used either as bare forward operating locations or as pre-stocked bases with fuel and ammunition. *RAFG*

Right:
Deliveries of the McDonnell Douglas/British Aerospace Harrier GR5 are due to begin in 1986, initially to RAF Germany. This new-technology aircraft has 11 stores attachments, two being used to carry the new Aden 25mm gun. *BAe*

Below right:
The British Aerospace Hawk is likely to play an increasingly important role as a tactical aircraft. Here demonstrating a weapon load of 4,800lb, it can operate over useful ranges with an external load of 6,800lb and retain considerable flight agility. A further asset is an extraordinarily small radar cross-section. *BAe*

Below:
Nuclear war may be 'unthinkable' but it is just another option where Soviet training is concerned. In such a situation NATO airbases would simply cease to exist, and NATO force commanders might wish they had instead used STOVL aircraft dispersed at pre-surveyed ski-jumps formed by the natural terrain, or mounted on trucks.

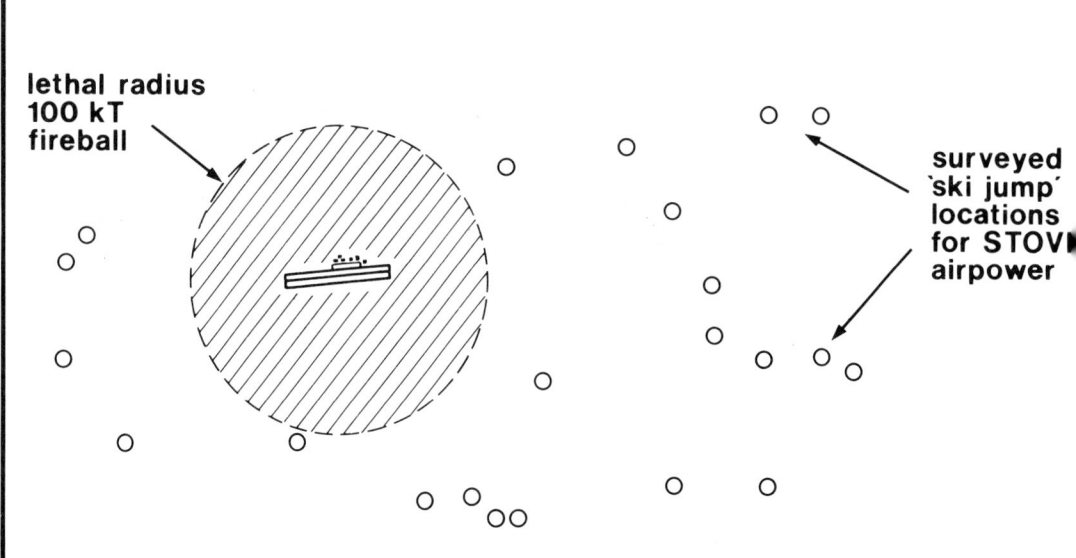

lethal radius
100 kT
fireball

surveyed
'ski jump'
locations
for STOVl
airpower

(864litre) drop tanks, and anti-radar chaff crudely stuffed in bundles under the airbrake and between the bombs and ejector racks. Today a properly schemed internal ECM suite is being added to all Harriers and Sea Harriers, there being just enough room in odd nooks and crannies. For the future the RAF Harrier force, deployed in two squadrons at the most easterly airfield on the Central Sector in Germany (Nos 3 and 4 at Gütersloh) and two units

in Britain, is to be updated with new systems, and later replaced from 1987 by the Harrier GR5. This is the British version of the AV-8B, which was developed mainly by McDonnell to carry a much greater bombload or fly twice as far. The RAF is buying 60 Mk 5s, and the order may rise to 100, and if none of the original Harriers is retired this would begin to add real muscle to the dispersable off-airfield airpower in NATO that would probably still be available on Day 2 of a future war. Of course, the US Marine Corps' much greater force of nine squadrons (306 initial full production aircraft) might well contribute to European defence. Meanwhile the Sea Harriers, brought back to an inventory strength higher than before 'Corporate' by 23 follow-on aircraft, to support an establishment of three front-line squadrons plus a training unit, will receive a major mid-life update after 1985 which will include a new Ferranti pulse-doppler radar giving complete look-down shoot-down capability, wingtip rails for AIM-9L or ASRAAM dogfight missiles, improved EW systems, and probably provision to use the AIM-120A missile in longer-range engagements.

Hawk

With transonic performance, and bombloads up to 6,800lb (3,085kg), the Hawk is an agile and formidable tactical aircraft, but in the NATO context even the original RAF Hawk T1 is of interest because it serves as a part-time home-defence interceptor. Strike Command has about 90 Hawks converted to carry the AIM-9L Sidewinder, and under current planning 72 will actually be equipped with two of these missiles to serve in the day interception role as well as weapons trainers. A more powerful single-seat attack version, Hawk 200, is being developed.

British Aerospace has modified almost 100 Hawks of the RAF to fire Sidewinder AAMs in the local-defence air combat role. This has proved a very successful mix, despite the fact the Hawk does not (in its T1 form) carry radar. Under present plans the RAF will actually load the missiles on 72 Hawks. This example is demonstrating the type's anti-ship capability, with a Sea Eagle missile. *BAe*

Armed with Sidewinder AAMs the BAe Hawk provides a valuable extra element in Britain's thinly spread air defence. This demo aircraft is also carrying a Sea Eagle anti-ship missile, up to four of which will be carried by the Buccaneers of Nos 12 and 208 Squadrons. *British Aerospace*

Customers around the world have purchased the Grumman Hawkeye as being the most cost/effective solution for their own airspace. It remains to be seen whether this opinion will also extend to NATO European countries, outside the coverage of the NAEW (NATO AEW) system. *Grumman*

Hawkeye

The Grumman E-2C remains in production at six per year to fill the US Navy's need for an early warning and command/control platform for sea control and maritime air defence, as explained in the next chapter. France has evaluated it for land-based AWACS use.

Jaguar

Developed jointly by Britain and France, this outstanding tactical attack and reconnaissance aircraft carries bombloads up to 10,500lb (4,763kg), which in the RAF Jaguar GR1 version can be delivered with fair accuracy in adverse conditions, though as in its standard form it lacks a forward-looking radar or terrain-following radar the Jaguar is not a true blind first-pass attack system. Advantages include large ground clearance and a long-stroke landing gear for off-airfield operation, though curiously this potentially vital capability appears not to be practised. Another is a passive RWR, but plans to fit internal countermeasures have not yet been carried out, nor has the erstwhile intention of replacing the excellent but small wing by a new design of deep supercritical form. RAF Germany had four squadrons (Nos 14, 17, 20 and 31) at Brüggen, plus No II (2) Squadron at Laarbruch which is also tasked in the tactical reconnaissance role carrying a belly sensor pod. In the UK are three further squadrons, Nos 6, 41 and 54, with No 41 being also equipped for reconnaissance. Jaguars have gradually been replaced by Tornado GR1s, beginning with the Brüggen wing, but the squadrons themselves are remaining Jaguar-equipped and merely being relocated back to Britain. The Jaguar is also the chief tactical attack aircraft of the French Armée de l'Air. Though not assigned to NATO, these are too potent not to mention. Of 200 total, including two-seaters, the last 30 were delivered with the Atlis II laser/TV pod for use in conjunction with smart weapons, initially the AS.30L. The Armée de l'Air has long-term update plans for all its Jaguars.

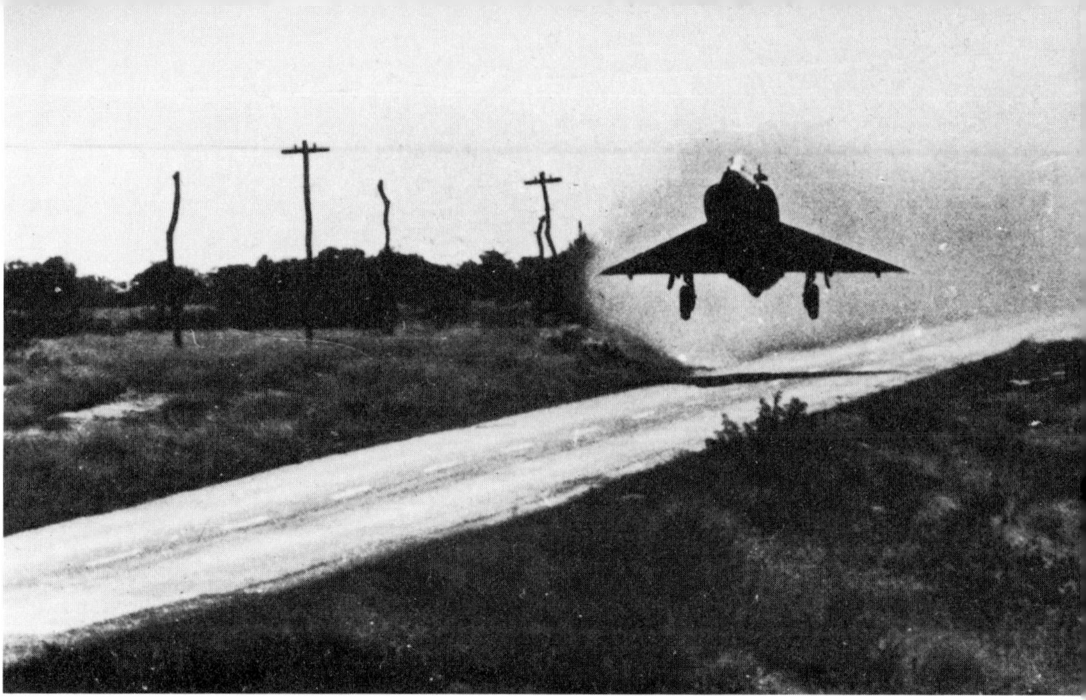

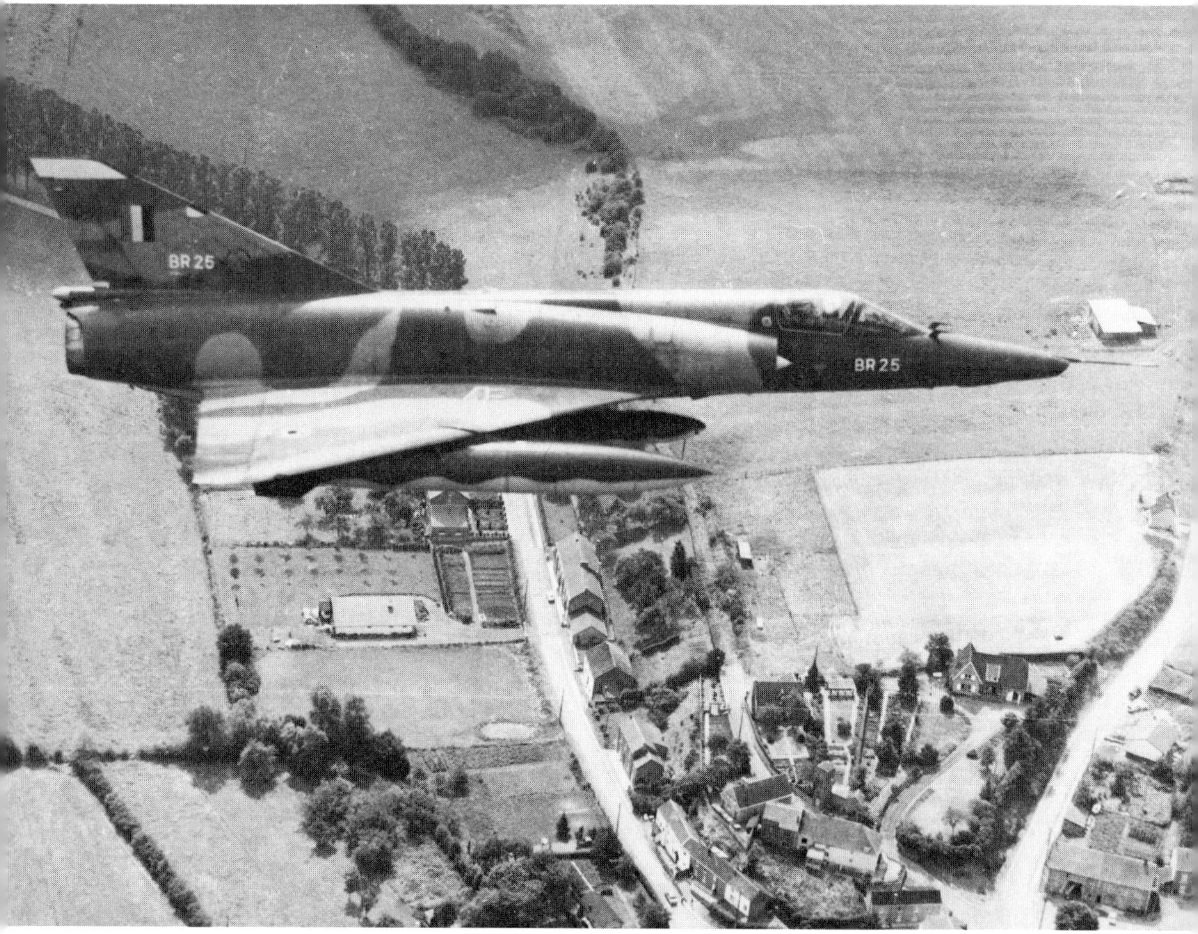
BR25
BR25

Mirage 5

The FAB (Belgian air force) still has a few Mirage 5BA tactical attack fighters, 5BR tactical reconnaissance aircraft and 5BD trainers, though all should be retired shortly after this book appears, the replacement being the vastly superior F-16.

Mirage F1

As well as being an important fighter in the French Armée de l'Air, the Mirage F1 serves with two NATO air forces, Greece and Spain. The basic type used by both nations is the F1.C, a multirole fighter and attack aircraft with a Cyrano IV radar. In the air interception role these are excellent aircraft, with good all-round flight performance and a choice of two 30mm guns, close-range Sidewinder or Magic missiles and medium-range R530 or Super 530 missiles. In the attack mission the F1.C has good flight performance, and over short ranges can carry a load of up to 4tonne (8,820lb) if no jammer pod is carried, but it lacks inertial navigation, terrain following and modern displays and weapon aiming. Some of these features are available in another variant, the ground-attack F1.E. Altogether the F1, even in the early C sub-type, is a tremendous improvement over the original delta-wing Mirage III, and various EW systems are available to customers including the Remora self-protection jammer which is linked with the basic Thomson-CSF Type BF passive RWR. Greece uses the F1.CG to equip 334 Squadron at Tanagra in the interception role. Spain's Ejercito del Aire uses the

F1.CE with two squadrons at Los Llanos in the
interception role, and the well-equipped F1.EE at
Gando (Canaries) in the non-nuclear strike role. In
emergency the latter unit would relocate to
continental Europe.

Nimrod

Though most Nimrods serve as oceanic patrol and
ASW aircraft, or (with No 51 Squadron RAF) as
dedicated Elint platforms, a special model, the
AEW3, is the RAF's first modern AWACS type
aircraft and this would play a central and potentially
crucial role in any European war. The AEW3 is
built around the totally new radar designed for this
task by Marconi Avionics, integrated with the
Cossor Guardsman IFF. The radar has many unique
or unusual features, one being interleaving of
high-PRF for surveillance of low-flying aircraft
with low-PRF for slow-moving targets such as
armour or ships. Another unusual feature is that the
aerial (antenna) system is split into two 180°
sectors, one at the nose of the aircraft and the other
at the tail. Obviously these have perfect radar
vision, unlike the rotodomes mounted on top of
large airframes as in other AWACS platforms, and
they are also pitch/roll stabilised against flight
manoeuvres and automatically compensate for the
cyclic errors present in other AWACS radars.
Operational service with RAF No 8 Squadron at
Waddington began in late 1984, and all 11 aircraft
should be in service by 1985. Their missions are

integrated both with the UKADGE ground system and with the NATO Sentry aircraft (see E-3 earlier in this chapter). The latter have multinational crews but use English throughout, and the computer software languages are compatible. Precise details of how the RAF's new AEW force will operate have not been disclosed, but there is no doubt that it will multiply the effectiveness and survivability of the entire RAF order of battle, and also that of most other NATO air forces on the central front.

Tornado IDS

With over 330 aircraft delivered by June 1984 this is fast becoming the No 2 NATO aircraft in terms of numbers, and as far as attack capability goes it is

Below:
NATO's AEW or AWACS aircraft comprise the E-3 Sentry (basically to USAF 'Core' standard) normally based at Geilenkirchen and the Nimrod AEW3 normally based at Waddington. They will collaborate by the JTIDS (Joint Tactical Information Distribution System). For the longer term the ideal platform would be based on the Airbus 310-300.

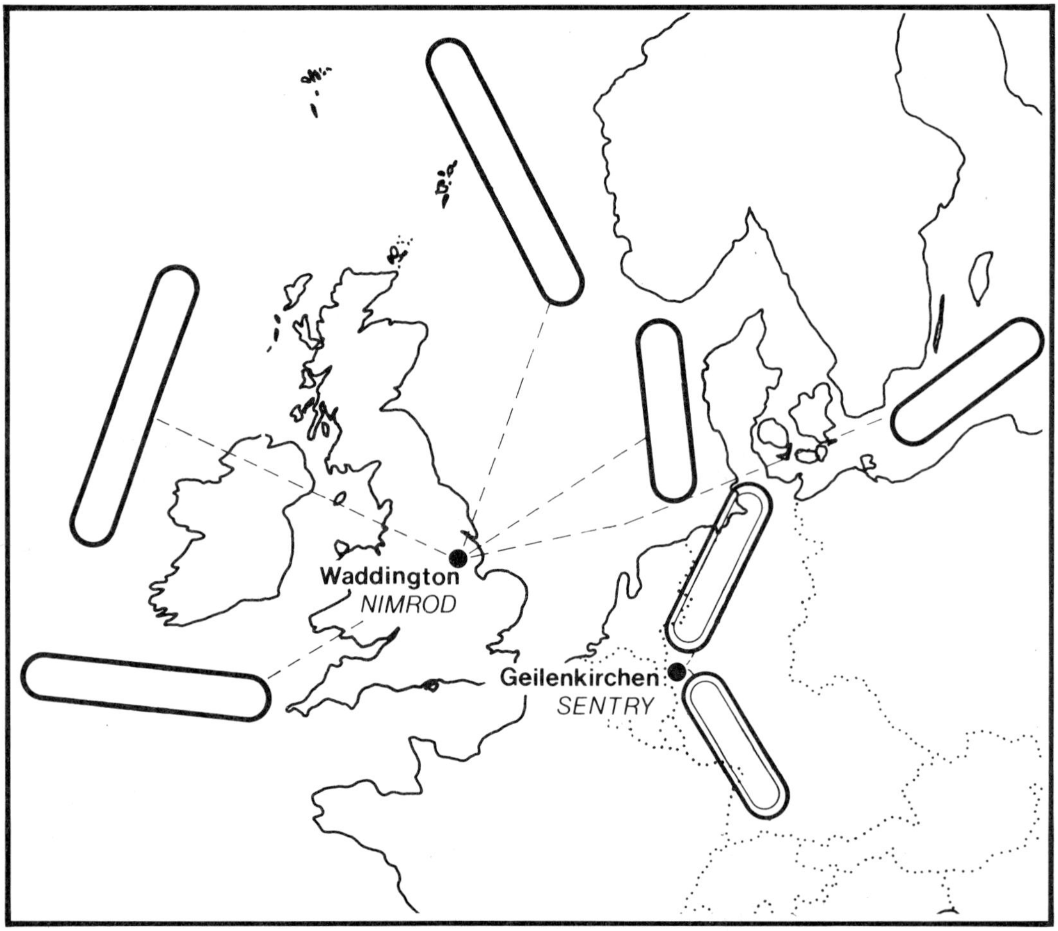

already No 1 by a clear margin. Designed to meet the requirements of the RAF, Luftwaffe, Marineflieger and AMI (Italian air force) the IDS (interdiction strike) version of the Tornado is the most capable aircraft of its size ever built. It does almost exactly the same job as the Soviet Su-24 'Fencer' but in a much smaller and more efficient airframe, burning roughly half as much fuel on each mission with its amazingly efficient and compact three-spool augmented turbofans. All IDS aircraft are similar except for slight differences in minor parts of the avionic fit, such as C^3 and the RWR/jammer installation. RAF Tornado GR1s use the new Sky Shadow jammer, while German and Italian examples usually carry the Zeus or Cerberus, plus a BOZ-100 chaff/flare dispenser pod. Fin-mounted threat warning gives all-round coverage, and at last with IDS Tornado even the RAF has an aircraft lacking nothing in EW

capabilities. The main radar is backed up by a TFR for flight at down to 100ft (30m) above undulating terrain, and a chisel fairing under the nose houses a laser for auto-acquisition of designated targets and super-accurate ranging. With a crew of two in tandem the cockpit workload is halved, and in any case the modern displays and the smooth ride (even at 800kt, 902mph, faster than any other aircraft in the world at sea level) make each crew-member's work seem almost simple. More weapons, of more types, can be carried than in any other tactical aircraft. For overland use more than 70 different types of store have been cleared for use, two of

Below:
A Tornado IDS of the Federal German Luftwaffe (GAF in NATO parlance) touching down at the TTTE (Tornado Tri-national Training Establishment) at RAF Cottesmore. This unique training school received its complement of 50 aircraft in 1982. Each of the three nations has its own weapon training unit. *BAe*

Bottom:
One of the flightlines at Cottesmore, where the first 800 pilots and navigators had been qualified as this book went to press, with the syllabus extended in 1983 to include automatic low-level terrain following by night. *BAe*

Above:
This happens to be a German aircraft, but nationalities of aircraft, instructor and pupil get all mixed up at the TTTE, to give 100% interoperability. It has been found that the qualities of the aircraft, which are mostly dual-pilot versions at TTTE, are such that the flight crew can almost ignore it and concentrate on the mission. *BAe*

special interest being the German MW-1 dispenser which fires bomblets or mines from both ends of 28 double-ended tubes in each of four tandem boxes carried under the fuselage, and the British JP233 which fires pavement-cratering or anti-armour bomblets and/or anti-personnel mines from two giant streamlined containers carried side-by-side under the fuselage. The first 150 aircraft delivered to the RAF went to the training unit at Cottesmore and the weapons training unit at Honington, followed by Nos 9 and 617 (ex-Vulcan) Squadrons. Then new squadrons were formed in RAF Germany, replacing the Brüggen Jaguar wing and Nos 15 and 16 (Buccaneer) Squadrons at Laarbruch. The two Marineflieger attack wings, MFG 1 and 2, have been converting from the F-104G, as also have 6° and 36° Stormi in Italy. In the Luftwaffe all four JaboG (fighter/bomber) wings, Nos 31 to 34, have either begun or

completed conversion from the F-104G. All use the Tornado in the battlefield interdiction, counter-air and close air support roles. Like all NATO airpower, the Achilles heel of the Tornado lies in its vulnerability to mass destruction on its combat-unit bases, which in early 1984 numbered just five. If this weakness could be eliminated, these aircraft would make a colossal difference to NATO airpower. In 1984 the Luftwaffe was discussing a follow-on purchase of a new ECR (electronic countermeasures and reconnaissance) version.

Tornado ADV
Designated Tornado F2 by the RAF, which was the original sponsoring customer, this air defence variant differs from the IDS in having a totally different radar, computer and software tailored primarily to the long-range interception mission. In order to accommodate tandem pairs of Sky Flash or Sparrow missiles recessed under the fuselage the length of the forward fuselage is increased by 53.5in (1.36m), which also enables internal fuel to be increased by 200gal (909 litres). The fixed wing glove (nib) is increased in chord and sweep to preserve the relationship between centre of lift and centre of gravity, and this has been made to reproduce the powerful behaviour of the original short nib as on the IDS. Other changes are that only one gun is fitted, and, instead of having provision

for a detachable inflight-refuelling probe unit as an excrescence on the right side of the forward fuselage, a very neat retractable probe is fitted as a permanent installation on the left side. Three prototype interceptors flew in 1979-80, and 18 production F2s are being delivered in the fourth Tornado production batch. No 19, the first of 52 in the fifth batch, is the first to have Mk 104 engines with slightly longer afterburners giving up to 15% extra afterburning thrust. Altogether the RAF will

Above:
Though it has structural provision for outboard wing pylons the Tornado F2 interceptor normally flies with four Sky Flash, two AIM-9L Sidewinders and two tanks. It has a single gun only, and compared with the IDS aircraft (which has an external pack on the right side housing a retractable probe) it has a permanently installed probe which retracts inside the nose on the left side. *BAe*

Right:
Precise speed figures for the interceptor Tornado have not yet been published, but it has been stated that speeds and accelerations of the early prototypes were superior to those of the IDS version, and that with extended jetpipes the figures were even higher. There is little doubt the production aircraft can catch anything else in the sky. *BAe*

probably receive 162 Tornado F2s, and there is no doubt these are the world's most formidable stand off all weather interceptors. The Foxhunter radar has a CW illumination mode to guide Sparrow and Sky Flash missiles, but later in the decade the AIM-120A AMRAAM will replace these earlier missiles and as this weapon dispenses with the CW mode it may be matched with an even more advanced coherent pulse doppler set. Foxhunter has great multimode capabilities, and to the existing ground-mapping mode it would be easy to add ground ranging and a laser for precise air/ground weapons delivery. In the initial deliveries in 1985 there will be a high proportion of AT (ADV trainer) aircraft with full combat capability but dual pilot controls. So important is the ADV that other NATO air forces are almost certain in due course to adopt it as a standard interceptor, with essentially the same attack capability as the IDS (though with small changes between missions). It is not intended as a dogfight aircraft, though it is no slouch and can certainly beat an F-4 in this role. Its ability to destroy all hostile aircraft from a distance will be virtually doubled with AIM-120A because the number of medium-range missiles carried will then probably be increased to eight, all being of the fire-and-forget type.

Below:
Tornado A03 in CAP configuration – four Sky Flash, two Sidewinders and two tanks. The production aircraft are finished in low-visibility pale grey. *BAe*

Bottom:
Fitted with RWR pods facing front and rear at the tail, XH168 is one of the Short-built Canberra PR9 aircraft formerly operated by RAF No 39 Squadron. These aircraft are now back at the maker's factory being completely reworked, one of the additions being a new stand-off side-looking radar as a UK counterpart to the TR-1. *Dave Thomas*

An Overview

It is doubtful that a single person outside the Warsaw Pact nations has ever considered it likely or even possible for the NATO countries to attack the Soviet Union or any of its partners in the WP alliance. Anything more pointless and suicidal would be difficult to imagine. NATO's entire existence is instead based on fear of an attack ordered by the Kremlin against the West.

The most common scenario is a giant push by the enormous and highly mobile WP armies from the frontier post at Helmstedt straight through to the Channel coast. If this were to be commanded by the Kremlin there is little doubt that, in a purely conventional war, it would result in a military defeat for NATO; how could we withstand 85 army divisions? It would in some ways be a re-run of May 1940, but with a very much greater disparity in strength between the opposing sides. Having come to this conclusion, it is equally important to suggest that such a campaign would at the same time be enormously costly to the WP forces.

Of course, if the Soviet Union began with a pre-emptive nuclear blow the result might be gained much more quickly. WP forces – all arms, by land, air and sea – are trained to fight in a total war, using not only conventional arms but also what they call REC (radio electronic combat) and nuclear, biological and chemical weapons. Constant realistic practice hones their skills in these terrifying new kinds of war, to the point where, while WP forces would still be effective, almost all NATO forces would be totally incapacitated and demoralised. But to engage in such a total war would be not only a disaster for the West but also a disaster for the East, because dozens of Soviet cities could be obliterated by the ICBMs, SLBMs and cruise missiles that survived the pre-emptive strike, if the US President chose to fire them. Not even the most aggressive and unpredictable Soviet leadership could believe such a war could be worthwhile.

One is inevitably left looking at the other ways in which the Soviet Politburo is continuously projecting Communist power around the world. The Kremlin has been so successful in its non-military

Above:
The US Army introduced Pershing 2 not – as the protest movement maintains – to exacerbate the nuclear situation but to enable warhead size to be dramatically reduced by increasing the terminal accuracy, by adding a nose guidance radar of a novel kind. Pershing 2 has been deployed in the Stuttgart area of West Germany. *US Army*

efforts that a European war begins to look like something that is not urgently needed. As seen from the Kremlin, the way things are going, Europe can be left to fall by itself. All that need be done at present is to keep up the pressure through the countless front organisations which manage the so-called 'peace movement'[1] to do everything possible to interfere with NATO's attempts to increase its ability to deter war and to defend itself. (We ought perhaps to remember what "Peace" means to the Soviet leadership; simple people in the West seem to think it means we all carry on as before, but Lenin defined it as "In the ultimate, it can only mean Communist world domination.") Here again success has been most gratifying: the names Cruise and Pershing are familiar to millions, but who can give the designations of the far larger and more numerous Soviet missiles?

Of course, if NATO's European members had no defences at all, then a Soviet takeover would be planned in a very short term indeed. Fortunately, the forces available to NATO are just about enough to cause substantial casualties to an invading force by land, sea and air – even after a devastating pre-emptive strike without any prior indications. For this reason, and only for this reason, the long-feared invasion from the east is not likely just as present. The Politburo has more urgent matters to attend to: mending fences with China, increasing the Soviet hold over the Middle East, Africa and Latin America, and continuously and relentlessly

Below:
Until 1984 NATO countries had no counterpart to the Soviet Union's formidable and growing forces of intermediate-range nuclear missiles. The map shows how the mobile SS-20 missiles, each with three independently targeted warheads, have been deployed right across the Soviet Union to menace not only Europe but also China and Japan. Those who shout 'No Cruise' ought perhaps to shout 'No SS-20'.

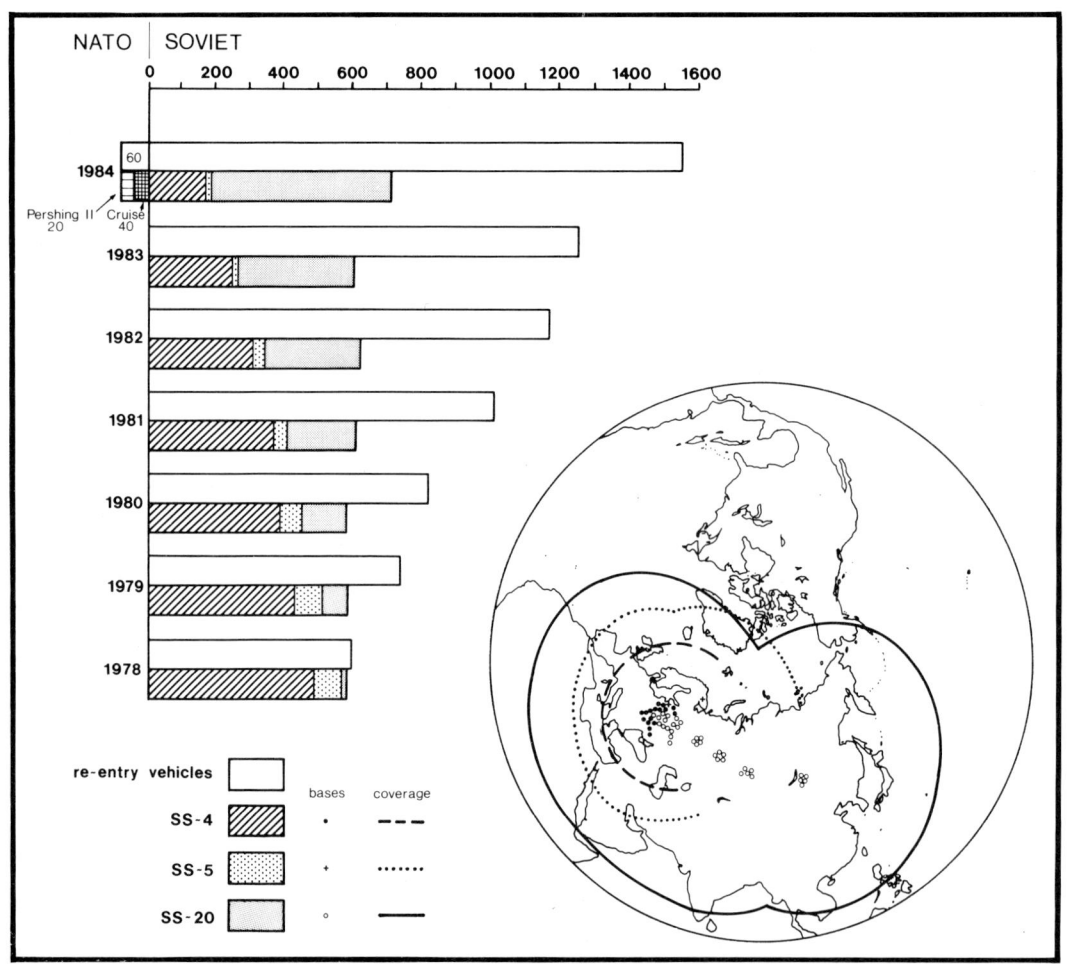

Top:
Called cruise by the protest movement, the TLAN (tactical land attack, nuclear) version of Tomahawk has been deployed in Europe in order to free the F-111 and Tornado from the nuclear interdiction task. The whole point of this mobile system is that, unlike the aircraft it replaces, it does not invite retaliation, because the enemy does not know where to aim. *GD via Janes*

Above:
Pictorial information on the awesomely prolific and capable SS-20 weapon system is so far virtually non-existent, so this American (Department of Defense) artist's impression is highly speculative. What is beyond dispute is that the missile is very mobile, and is usually dispersed in local groups of nine. The usual payload is believed to be three warheads each of 150KT yield, the Soviet figure for range being 4,000-4,500km (2,485-2,796 miles). *DoD*

increasing its already terrifying military might, especially in the deployment of mass-destruction nuclear and chemical systems.

So large is the Soviet capability in nuclear and chemical weapons that their sheer numbers could, taken in conjunction with the colossal Soviet expenditure on greater hardening and increased ABM (anti-ballistic missile) defences, take away the ability of the American ICBM and SLBM forces to deter aggression. When the chips are down, armaments are a matter of money, and there is no way that the governments of the free and open Western democracies are going to match the weapons expenditure of the Soviet Union. In some areas, such as civil defence, most NATO countries not only have no defence but no possibility of providing one – not because they fail to perceive a threat but because the threat is so large that the population in general would rather pretend it did not exist.

It is partly because Cruise and Pershing attempt to rectify an incredible imbalance of forces that the Soviet leadership has reacted so violently against them. Many ordinary people in the NATO countries – indeed, throughout the world – are unaware of the fact that facing the Soviet SS-4, SS-5 and SS-20 long-range INF (intermediate-range nuclear force) missiles there has in the past been not one single NATO missile. Even the planned deployment of 464 ground-launched cruise missiles and 108 Pershing 2s looks puny in comparison with known Soviet deployments, and the figures shown in an accompanying graphical plot are probably underestimates because SS-20 is a highly mobile weapon, which can quickly be driven off a highway and into a forest, and the NATO strength assessments are probably underestimates.

It is a further reflection on the frightening contrast between NATO's weakness and the Soviet Union's strength to note that only the Soviets have comprehensive defence against missile attack. As previously noted, enormous installations have been built in the Soviet Union for 19 years to counter any ICBM attack. Now a new missile called SA-12 has begun to be deployed throughout the NATO Central Sector, initially in East Germany, and as well as having very high capability against all aircraft (and, presumably any cruise missile or RPV in this region) it is said to have a primary role as an ABM to destroy Pershing 2 missiles in flight. Said to be basically a land-based version of the new and very powerful SA-N-6 missile that provides the chief air defence of the surface warship *Kirov*, SA-12 apparently has exceptionally fast reaction to any threat, and both very high flight performance and great accuracy, good enough to destroy a hypersonic warhead.

In contrast, NATO has quite a lot of modern combat aircraft, manned by skilled and courageous

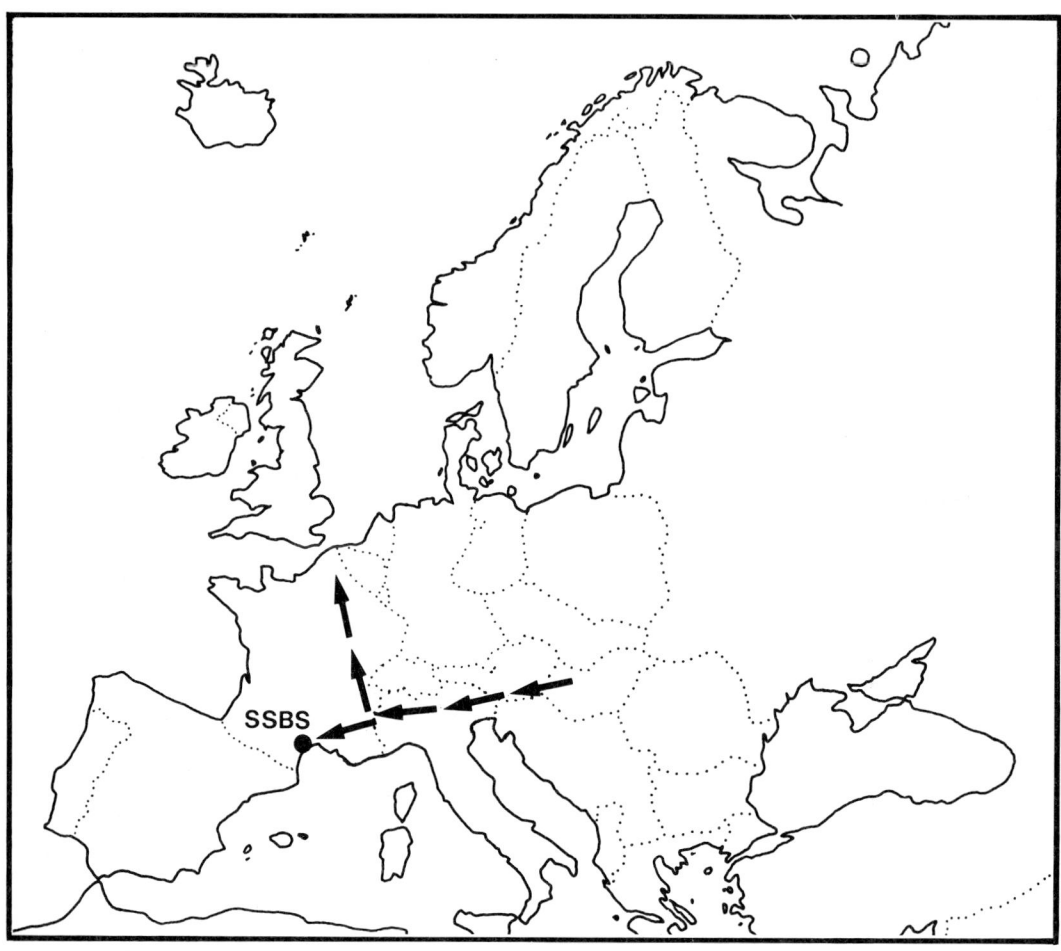

Above:
The main thrust of a Warsaw Pact invasion of Western Europe might pass south of the Alps. It could rapidly link up with airborne forces dropped on the French SSBS silos before turning north.

pilots, and despite the world's greatest-ever numbers of anti-aircraft defences throughout the WP region opposite the Central Front, these would give a good account of themselves in war if they survived destruction of their bases. Even in defence against an air armada from the east NATO is far from defenceless, and it is for these reasons that the impartial observer is bound to conclude that a head-on conflict in Europe is the last thing the Kremlin wishes. It is almost the only military adventure where, though the outcome might be satisfactory, the price would be very high indeed. The Russians are logical in their thinking, and prefer to gain their objectives by the least-costly methods.

There are other considerations to a military takeover of Western Europe. The countries occupied must be left as little damaged as possible if they are to be of maximum use, yet the residual populations must somehow be suppressed, and deterred from guerrilla activity, using the minimal numbers of occupying forces. What about the rest of the world? The Socialist countries have always preached that they merely defend themselves, and that it is the Capitalists who are the aggressors. How could a bloody invasion of Western Europe be made to look like pure defence against Western aggression? Whilst thus engaged, might the Soviet Union be stabbed in the rear by China? Most important of all, how could the Kremlin be certain that the deterrent power of the USA – which may be mainly ancient, but it still works – would not be used? Could a mere blunt threat – 'You destroy Moscow and we'll destroy New York' – actually force the US President to wring his hands in impotent despair as Europe went under?

All these questions have caused many furrowed brows, and are hardly new. However extremely unlikely it may be – while NATO still has strong air forces – a European air war is not totally impossible, and that is what this book is about.

The Plan
We in the West know that the VGK, the Soviet supreme high command, has drawn up several basic plans for the takeover of the rest of Europe. Some of them may have looked so promising that they have been refined in detail and taken to the point at which all that was needed was a single telephoned instruction. But if the 'balloon were to go up', the defenders in the West would not know what the plan was – unless intelligence was amazingly good or lucky. Apart from massive pre-emptive strikes we cannot guess in advance at its content, and this inevitably constrains how one predicts the course of a future air war.

In general the area that matters is the Central Sector. Here is a straight run through to the Channel coast, which would in a matter of hours eliminate Federal Germany, take over what was left of the Ruhr and many other important manufacturing, mining and research centres, and split the remainder of NATO into almost helpless regions to the north and south which could be mopped up more or less at leisure. On the other hand, this is the most commonly assumed scenario, so it is where NATO has most of its strength. NATO's military commanders have always been even more worried about the Northern and Southern Regions, where there is far more terrain to defend and far fewer defence forces, except in that Greece and Turkey have armies which are large by NATO standard, though poorly equipped with any modern weapons. Whichever way the NATO general looks, the situation appears very alarming.

Any thrust to the West would be to some degree a race against time, because it would be desirable to get the job done before many US troops could be flown in from the USA, and certainly before troopships from that country could dock at Continental ports. This being so, a thrust through Scandinavia, or in the Balkans, appears merely a waste of time (though such an attack would certainly be mounted as a diversion, to tie up as much as possible of the NATO firepower). The main attack surely has to be through the Central Region, and if Federal Germany looks too difficult to invade the obvious alternative is the fastest possible buildup in Hungary and a thrust with 50 divisions through Austria and northern Yugoslavia, northern Italy and southern France, backed up by a massive air-drop and seaborne landing in southern France. The air-drop would be right on top of the Armée de l'Air SSBS missile silos, eliminating their nuclear threat (the only one anywhere in Western Europe) before the crews knew what was happening. Once the main force had penetrated well into France it could turn right, through Lyon and Dijon and pass east of Paris to the Channel. A smaller thrust could link with the air/sea invaders and head for Bordeaux.

Such a plan must have been carefully studied by NATO staffs, so it could hardly hope to catch them completely off-balance, but it probably would cause massive upheavals in the NATO forces and large geographical redispositions. The spearhead would almost certainly move much faster than in a direct crossing of Federal Germany, and the WP ground forces are so powerful that, a few days after the start of the war, when the leading troops were heading into northern France from the south, a second and equally big thrust could drive straight through Germany to meet only the resistance of those few troops still in that country. This would be the biggest pincer movement of all time, with Switzerland completely untouched in the middle.

It is thus obvious that the VGK would plan a war of movement that would make Hitler's Blitzkrieg look positively snail-like. Compared with the armour and supporting vehicles that swarmed into Belgium and France on 10 May 1940 today's WP armoured and motor/rifle divisions actually drive only slightly faster, and even if not in contact with the enemy it is doubtful if the whole force could sustain better than 20mph (32km/hr). Where it scores is in the ability to maintain speeds of this order even well away from highways – which would be choked by civilian refugees – and to drive straight across rivers with full amphibious capability. The only WP spearhead vehicles that are not amphibious are, of course, the very heavy main battle tanks, and these can ford with snorkels to a water depth of 18ft (5.5m). We may take it for granted that the exact crossing places of all the rivers have been selected already. Great attention has been paid to precise navigation with a fast-moving army, using inertial and satellite guidance, so it is doubtful that local Communist agents will be needed to put radio beacons at key locations.

In many ways it is easier for attack aircraft to hit a moving army than a fixed one. A moving army is much more likely to emit radio signals and heat (infra-red), and many modern aircraft radars have MTI (moving-target indication) which clearly picks a moving object out from the stationary background. On the other hand many MTI circuits have deliberately been modified so that they can 'see' low-flying aircraft, including helicopters, whilst showing no interest in land vehicles. A case in point is the excellent Hughes APG-63 radar (now updated and improved, with reprogrammable software and a large memory) in the F-15C Eagles of the USAF 36th TFW based at Bitburg, Federal Germany. The 36th is naturally tasked with trying to shoot down WP aircraft, and most of these are

DBS (doppler beam sharpening) to give a photographic sharpness to the ground picture which in night or bad-weather conditions can be a great advantage. Now we have the SAR (synthetic-aperture radar), which behaves as if it had an aerial (US = antenna) hundreds of feet across, thus giving the best picture of all.

Moreover, though the first SARs were being built in the early 1980s for reconnaissance aircraft, Grumman and Norden have used the same technique in a stunningly simple and low-cost way to build what they consider to be the best attack radar yet. Norden has for many years supplied the radars for A-6 Intruder attack aircraft, and to turn this regular APQ-148 radar into that needed for tomorrow's RGWS (radar-guided weapon system) needs only modest additions, the main one being an interferometer, plus a new invention called a relative-angle processor. The latter studies the relative speeds at which ground targets appear to be moving relative to the aircraft – fastest dead ahead, and zero when directly abeam – and turns the measured 'doppler shift', or apparent change in

Above:
Capts Howard L. Pope Jr and Fred Bell, from the 36th TFW at Bitburg, Germany, study the new and rapidly reprogrammable radar of the F-15C which, when it is finished, will replace their present F-15A. The upgraded Eagles are also replacing the original version at the 32nd TFS, Camp New Amsterdam, in the Netherlands. *MCAIR*

Below:
One of the basic principles behind the RGWS (radar-guided weapon system) is that the relative velocity of the target (a bridge, office building and factory are shown) varies from zero up to the groundspeed of the aircraft, depending on the target's bearing at any instant. After using a high-resolution SAR to locate its target the aircraft can then fire radar-guided missiles in a fire-and-forget mode. Each RGWS missile is individually locked on to its own small target, on which it dives from above. The operator in the RGWS aircraft retains a considerable measure of command; for example, if he is not satisfied the weapon is on target he may decide not to arm it. *Grumman*

expected at very low altitudes. In the look-down shoot-down mode, which is the only one that can be used in such missions, the radars were persistently locking-on to BMW and Mercedes cars speeding along the Autobahns, so the circuits were modified to cut out all traffic at less than 120mph (193km/hr). Not even the most enthusiastic WP ground-forces driver is going to make any impression on the radars of the 36th (though the F-15s would have their hands full with aerial targets anyway).

Air-to-ground attack radars have never ceased to be improved for 40 years, and the remarkable thing is that dramatic new advances are being announced almost annually. Digital signal processing was one of the greatest, though at first (in the early 1970s) the processing was hard-wired in and could not readily be altered. Then came the reprogrammable processors in the late 1970s, together with the first

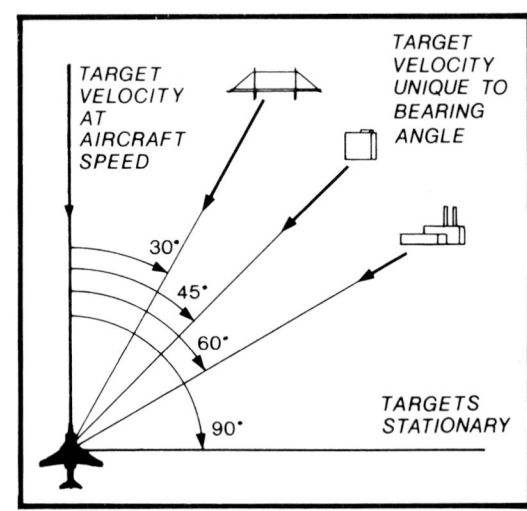

frequency of the reflected signals, into precise angular measures to indicate exactly where each target is. It can handle not only a truck driving along a straight road but also the pitching and swaying of a tank crossing rough ground, or a frigate in a rough sea, and still give an exact result. It is not put off by the often very fast movement of leaves blowing in a gale, or spray blown from the tops of waves, and it is also inherently highly resistant to hostile countermeasures.

Acquisition and classification of every important surface target is just the beginning of the new radar's task. Previous radars could be incapacitated if an invading army simply stopped moving and switched off all electronic emitters. This often happened in Vietnam. The new radar can spot individual targets, such as trucks, scores of miles away, and store the information on each target in its memory. If necessary it can indicate the moving targets in a distinctive colour. It makes no difference if the enemy drivers take fright and stop; the target remains stored in the memory as one that had been moving, and its colour stays unchanged. It cannot escape whatever weapon is coming to it.

The RGWS next moves into the attack phase. To start with, as soon as they are within range, all the friendly (NATO) aircraft let go their air-to-air missiles, in the general direction of the enemy army. Then they all wheel away and head for home as fast as possible, hopefully without ever coming within effective range of any of the WP defences, not even the SAMs. This would probably preclude the use of unpowered missiles, such as Walleye; self-powered cruise weapons are needed, and they head for their targets on a cheap strapdown inertial system or simple mid-course autopilot. Most of the missiles could be launched by simple, cheap attack aircraft with no radar, laser, FLIR or any other weapon-aiming system. All they have to do is fly with an RGWS aircraft and let go the missiles at about the same time.

When the missiles are half-way to their target the RGWS aircraft switches on its radar and selects the

Below:
While the Fairchild Republic A-10A was deliberately planned as an 'austere' aircraft – a euphemistic way of saying badly equipped with all-weather avionics – its size and lifting ability makes it ideally suited to progressive updating with avionics to protect it from destruction and assist it in hitting the enemy. Already the USAF is taking its first halting steps down this path. *USAF*

'one scan' mode. The radar makes just one lightning-fast sweep of the battlefield, too fast for any countermeasures to affect it. In that brief moment of time the single scan updates the positions of all the targets and all the missiles, allowing a midcourse correction if required. With 35sec to go, the RGWS radar is again switched on, but this time in the high-resolution SAR mode. The operator in the RGWS aircraft (which should be a two-seater, though the pilot could just about cope) then studies the targets. He can pick out every truck, every tank, every self-propelled gun or SAM vehicle – or, if it is a large warship, he can actually pick out the spots where he wants the missiles to hit. Small crosshairs are placed over each target, greatly magnified on the display in the aircraft even though the latter is now many miles distant. As each missile comes on to the screen it is automatically commanded to stabilise dead-centre in each set of cross-hairs. At a predetermined point warheads – probably of the cluster type – rain down directly above each individual target. The value of RGWS as a force-multiplier, especially in the precision guidance of missiles released by simple 'unequipped' attack aircraft such as the A-10A, cannot be overemphasised.

Though the original RGWS radar was carried by an A-6 of the US Navy, the main result for land warfare is likely to come out of the Pave Mover programme, most of the testing of which has been done with an F-111A, as noted earlier. Though the F-111A was the world's most advanced attack aircraft in the mid-1960s, today the basic aircraft is lacking in precision weapon-delivery systems, and

Below:
In this highly stylised impression the Boeing artist has identified the USAF Pave Mover platform as the E-8, though this designation is still speculative. Based on surplus 707-320s, the Pave Mover would serve a powerful C^3 (command/control/communication) role using as chief sensor a multi-mode SAR (synthetic aperture radar) with MTI (moving-target indication) to find and locate every kind of target. This E-8 is collaborating with an E-3 and B-52. *Boeing*

Right:
Hughes Aircraft produced 28,000 of the original AGM-65A and B models of Maverick, which today arm almost all USAF tactical aircraft. This photo sequence shows the effect of a hit on a concrete runway by the new AGM-65E Laser Maverick, which with good laser designation of the target can put its 300lb blast/frag warhead on precisely the commanded spot. *Hughes*

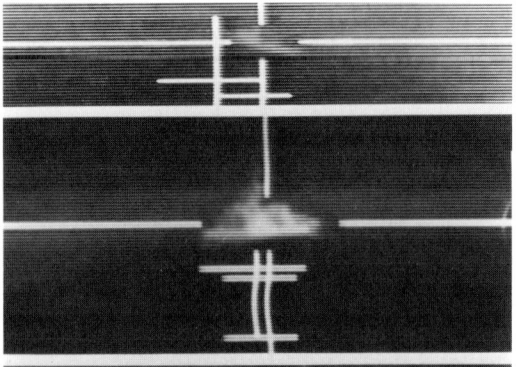

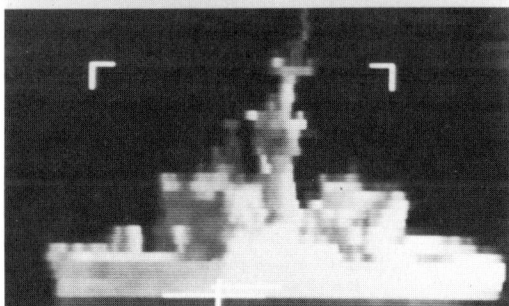

Right:
The USAF PLSS (Precision Location/Strike System) is one of several schemes for providing round-the-clock all-weather attack capability, especially against emitting targets. TR-1s would collect the data.

Left:
Another new Maverick is AGM-65F, which like the D version has IIR guidance. This sequence shows the growth in size of USS *Bagley* as seen on the cockpit display as an AGM-65F homes in. The first picture was taken at a time when the ship was far beyond the visual range of the aircraft crew. *Hughes*

Below:
Externally indistinguishable from a TR-1A, this is a Lockheed U-2R, a monster sensor platform derived from the much smaller earlier U-2 versions of the 1950s. Special payloads are carried in the fuselage and wing pods, looking down from heights of around 80,000ft. *Lockheed*

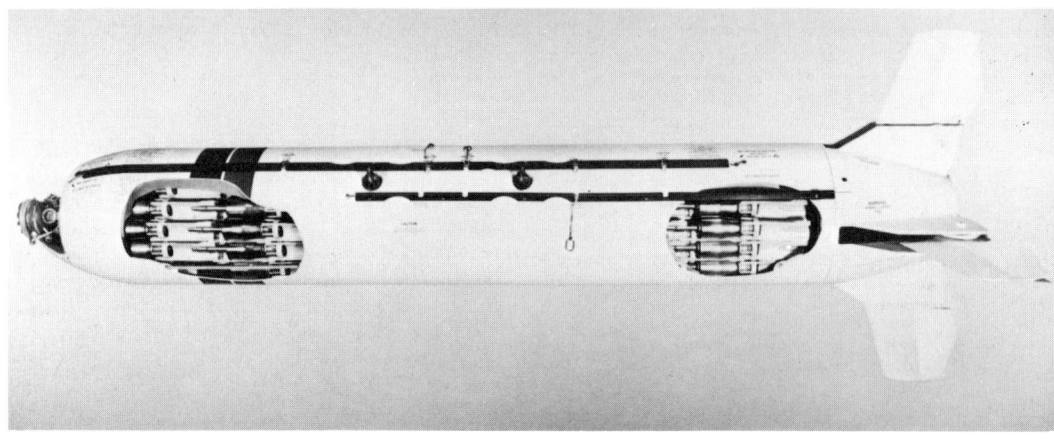

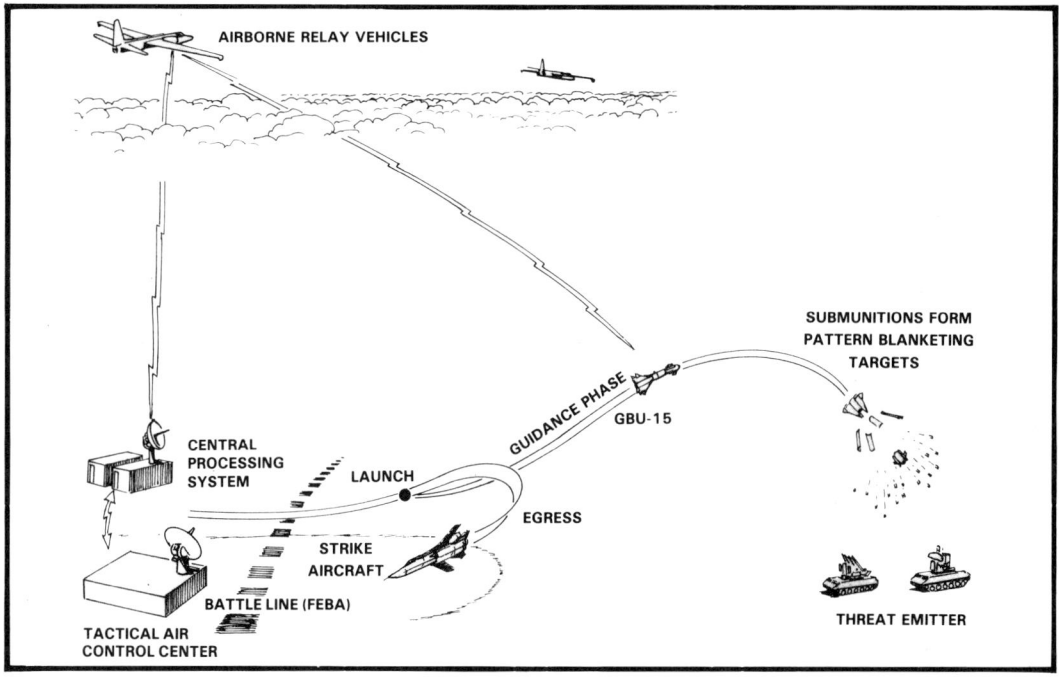

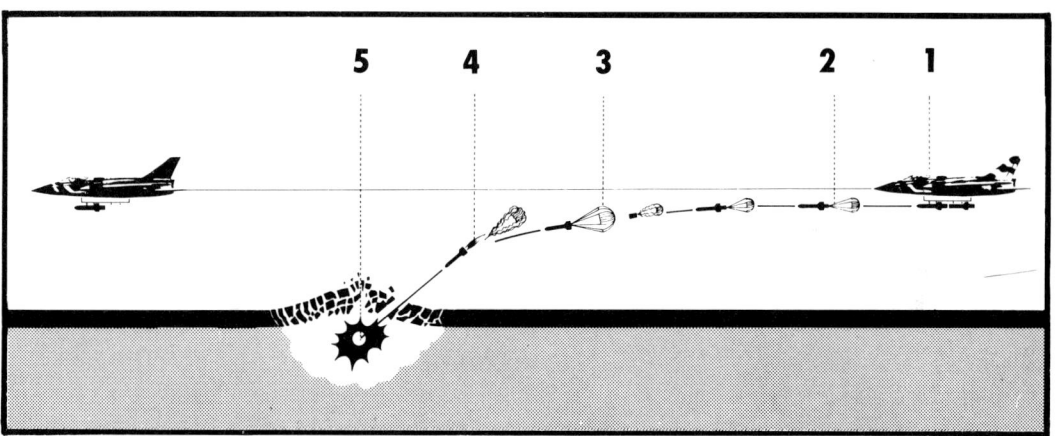

Left:
Manufactured in very large numbers, the Rockeye series are the most common American cluster bomb dispensers. This anti-armour version contains 246 hollow-charge bomblets, visible through the openings cut in the casing for display purposes.
Marquardt

Above:
Pictured on an earlier page carried by a Mirage F1.A, the Matra Durandal is used in large numbers to crater airfield runways and hardstandings. It has also demonstrated its ability to destroy aircraft inside HASs. *Matra*
1 Release of the bomb, locking of parachutes, and initiation of the firing sequence.
2 Deployment of deceleration parachute
3 Separation of the first parachute and deployment of the main parachute; pyrotechnic alignment after

check of correct parachute operation.
4 Jettison of the main parachute and ignition of the rocket motor.
5 Penetration and explosion after a firing delay.

Pave Mover gives both it and almost any other NATO aircraft tremendous new capability. This capability even surpasses that planned with many cancelled systems costing much more, and when combined with the dispensed submunition concept which is at the heart of the Assault Breaker project the results are dramatic. Assault Breaker, managed by the US DARPA (Defense Advanced Research Projects Agency), was specially intended to defend battlefields against large numbers of enemy armoured vehicles by firing much greater numbers

of small bomblets, called submunitions. Some could be air-launched, but most would fired from guns or carried in self-propelled 'bus' vehicles. Guidance systems, such as the USAF Pave Mover radar, could provide precision homing on to each enemy tank.

Several European NATO nations have their own research projects for precision guidance of dispensed submunitions, but American hardware is likely to become standard. In the same way, for the clear reasons of funding limitations, interoperability and standardisation, it is probable that American

EW systems (both defensive and offensive) and weapon-aiming systems (such as LANTIRN) will be used very widely throughout NATO. As always, the problem is money.

Recognition in the NATO capitals of the frightening situation that confronts the Alliance at present is enabling a steady effort to be maintained to update the tactical air forces and improve their ability to communicate with each other and to penetrate enemy airspace, but even the manned-aircraft war as publicised appears to leave many questions unanswered. Much more seriously, nothing at all has been said about defending Western Europe against the formidable and rapidly growing force of Soviet ballistic missiles, against which no known NATO weapons have much effectiveness.

To deal with the NATO manned-aircraft scene first, in any European war the airspace would become extremely crowded. The planned C^3 systems will be vital, but what about the vulnerability of the aircraft themselves? Those at treetop height may have some chance of survival, but the TR-1 surveillance machines and the AWACS platforms will be at altitudes between 29,000ft (for the latter) and perhaps 75,000ft (for the TR-1), where they will stand out very clearly on all the front-line WP air-defence systems. Quite apart from their vulnerability to WP interceptors, an equally serious threat is posed by such SAM

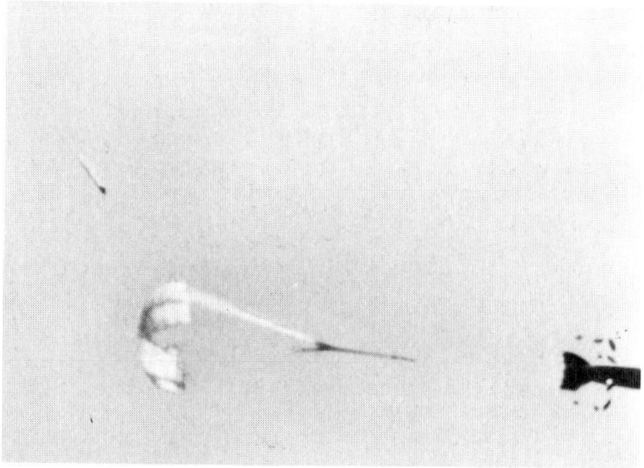

Above.
Photo sequence showing the operation of Beluga, in this instance dropped from a Mirage III. First the bomb is retarded by a parachute to enable the aircraft to clear the area; then the 151 submunitions are dispensed at a controlled rate and individually braked. *Matra*

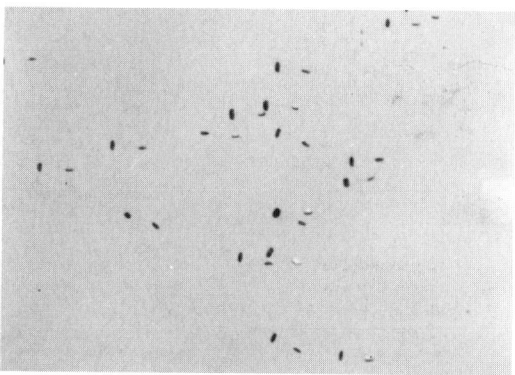

systems as SA-4 'Ganef' and SA-5 'Gammon', backed up by rapidly growing numbers of the system which NATO calls SA-10. The SA-5 was originally a giant fixed-base system to defend Soviet cities, but since 1979 a vast chain of SA-5 installations has been constructed from the Baltic to Czechoslovakia, running the entire length of the NATO Central Sector. By early 1983 the chain was complete except for two gaps in Hungary which were being filled by round-the-clock site construction. According to a Western report, each site provides a large overlap in coverage with its neighbours, assuming the usual missile range at all levels of 180 miles (290km). Against high-flying targets, range is about 200 miles (322km). So large is the SA-5 system that these are fixed installations. All other WP SAM systems except SA-10 (which is being made mobile) are designed to travel across country with the ground forces. Their range against high-altitude targets is about 45 miles (over 70km) for SA-4 and at least 62 miles (100km) for SA-10. This is further than the distance TR-1 can see

Right:
A new-generation weapon by Hunting, JP233 is
Britain's chief new low-altitude airfield attack
system. It comprises a container, of various sizes
and shapes, into which is packed submunitions of
two types, the SG357 for runway cratering and the
HB876 for area-denial. The Tornado carries two
installations at the front of the body pylons
containing 430 Type HB876 followed by two larger
rear containers holding 60 SG357s. *BAe*

Below:
In peacetime Lockheed TR-1 aircraft, normally
operating from RAF Alconbury, maintain
surveillance of Warsaw Pact territory from a patrol
area on the NATO side of any frontier. Similar
surveillance is planned to be provided by the British
Army's CASTOR (Corps Airborne Stand-Off Radar)
carried either by six to nine Canberras based in
Britain or about 15 Turbo-Islanders based in West
Germany.

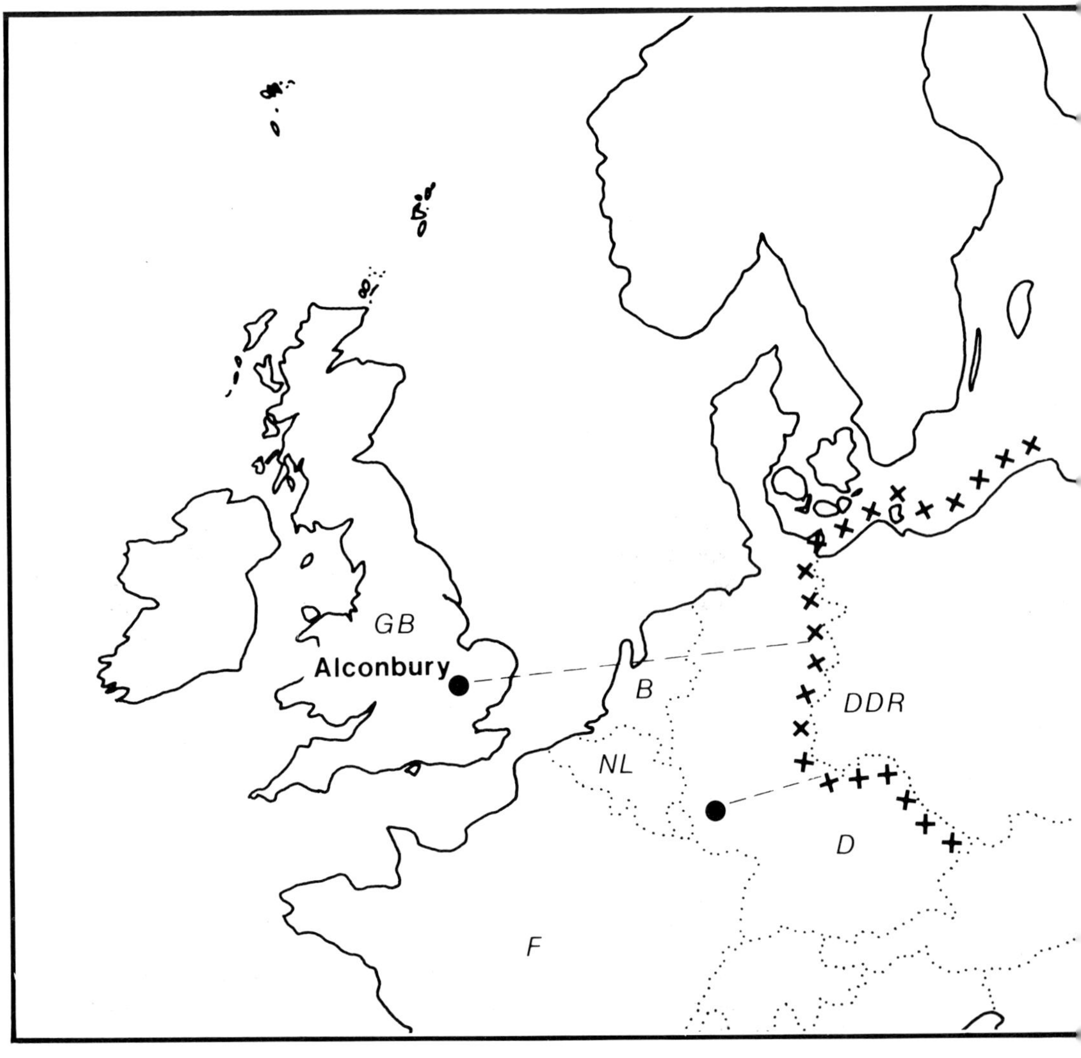

GB

Alconbury

B

NL

DDR

D

F

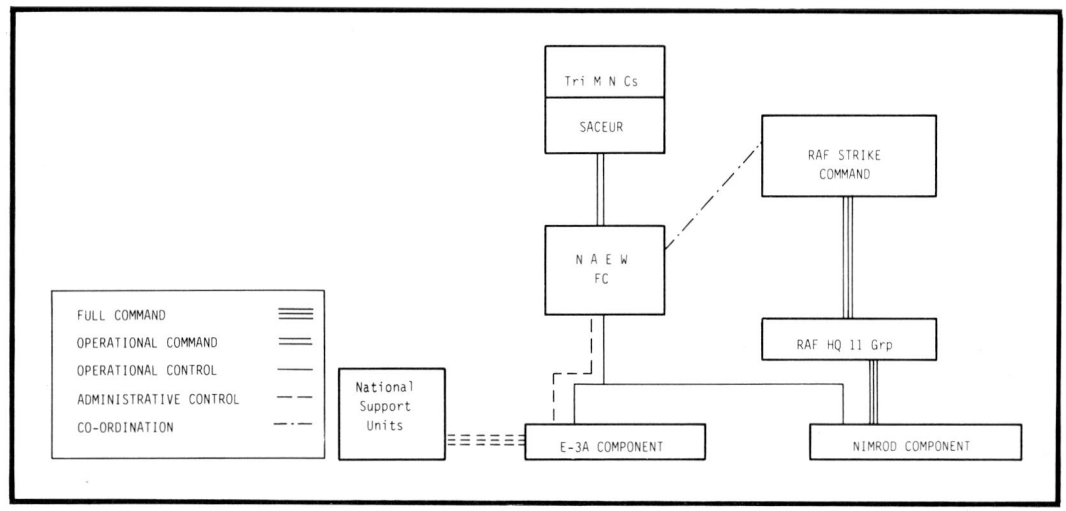

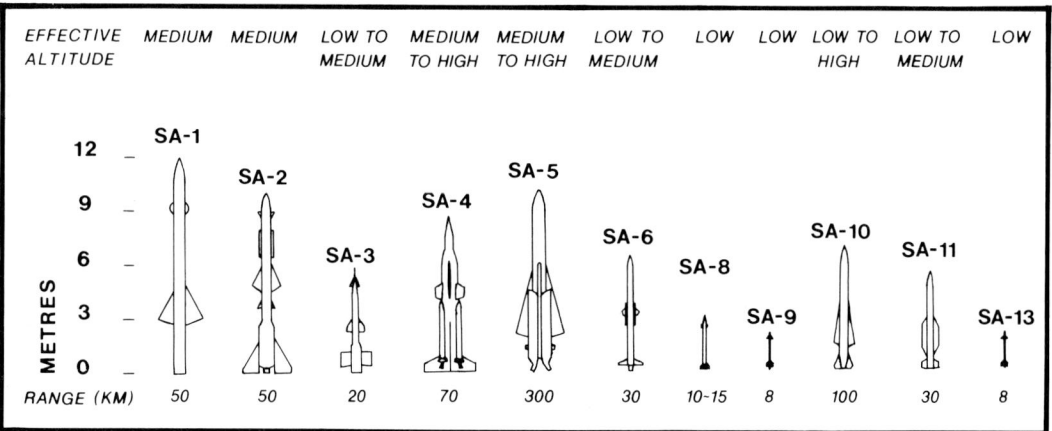

Top:

Though RAF Strike Command retains 'full command' of its Nimrod AEW force (No 8 Squadron based at Waddington), in practice operational control is exercised by NAEW FC (NATO AEW Force Commander, in 1984 Maj-Gen Leighton Palmerton) who in turn is responsible through Supreme Allied Commander Europe to the three MNCs (Major NATO Commanders).

Above:

The Soviet air-defence forces deploy more SAMs than all the rest of the world combined. Particular effort has been spent on the large SA-10 weapon system which is believed to have the capability of destroying aircraft or missiles at any altitude. This system is progressively replacing the SA-1 around Moscow.

laterally with its sensors, and it would be an almost impossible task to protect a TR-1 against such weapons.

The AWACS platforms, initially the E-3A/B Sentry and Nimrod, are extremely sophisticated aircraft which contain considerable electric generation power and have plenty of available payload. There would be little difficulty in equipping them with dispensed chaff and IR decoys, and it might be possible to install very high-power active jammers (of course, with effective power management and directional control so that they really did some good) without interfering with the vital radar and IFF system which is the reason for their existence. Nothing has been said about how these crucial aircraft would actually stay alive, and the author doubts that they could either protect themselves with the systems just described or even sustain such defences over the 6 to 10 hours of a combat mission. All diagrams of AWACS deployment so far published show the pattern being flown lying directly above the major air activity. In war this would clearly be impossible, and little has been said about how well these aircraft could fulfil their duties if offset 100 miles (161km) to the rear of the FEBA (forward edge of the battle area, now often called FLOT, for forward line of troops).

Above:

With all 18 E-3A/NATO Sentry aircraft delivered, the hardstanding at Geilenkirchen is crowded. The 15 men making up the crew for each mission are drawn variously from Belgium, Canada, Denmark, West Germany, Greece, Italy, the Netherlands, Norway, Portugal, Turkey and the USA. Every, repeat every, decision on the base has to be agreed by the 11 nations. The lone RAF liaison officer does not have to be involved. *RAFG*

Top right:

Many thousands of these SAMs, called SA-3 'Goa' by NATO, are deployed by all WP countries, and many others. A tandem-boosted canard, it reaches out to about 45,000ft but is used chiefly against low-level aircraft. This quad launcher is the current WP standard, replacing the pattern illustrated in Chapter 1. *Tass*

Centre right:

Though the numbers are gradually declining the almost prehistoric V750VK guided missile system, called SA-2 'Guideline' by NATO, continues to be important because of its sheer numbers. Used by every WP country (and many others), there are numerous versions and progressive updates. *Tass*

Below right:

One of the most formidable SAMs is the fully mobile (air-portable and amphibious) system called SA-4 'Ganef' by NATO, and widely deployed by Soviet forces as well as army divisions in Czechoslovakia and East Germany. Weighing about 4,000lb, the ramjet missile can reach to 44 miles at any height up to 80,000ft. *Tass*

Of course, as the AWACS concept has been known for 15 years, one must assume that a Soviet weapon system to counter it has been under development for the same period. The most obvious guidance method would be a purely passive one, to home on the lighthouse-like radiation from the target. So far as is known, there is no such thing as a passive AWACS; it has to do its job by active radar, so a specially tailored SAM would have plenty of signal power to home on to. It is inconceivable that spread-spectrum frequency-hopping techniques could effectively counter a modern missile designed to home on the emissions from the APY-1 radar, the characteristic signatures of which are certainly supplied to the Soviet Union on a daily basis. As for the carrier vehicle, more than 20 years ago the USAF had IM-99B Bomarc, a cruise-type SAM with an effective range against a high-altitude target of 440 miles (over 700km), and today we could obtain any range we wish, and without using wings. (For example, another US missile of a bygone era, the Spartan, was capable of destroying small ICBM warheads at ranges out to 465 miles (750km). Vulnerability of the AWACS platforms cannot have been overlooked, and it would be ridiculous for NATO planners to have based their calculations on such irrelevant Soviet SAMs as SA-2 or SA-6, but one wonders just what magic these extremely costly aircraft can perform to keep the warheads away?

This question has been examined because there

are never going to be very many AWACS aircraft, or many TR-1s or NKC-135 relay aircraft, or E-6 Tacamos or any other of the special-purpose NATO platforms used in C^3 roles. The loss of a single one would have large and immediate repercussions on the whole air battle, and to a slightly lesser degree on the land and sea battle as well. These are the aerial targets that the WP forces will be most eager to destroy, and the ones that it will be impossible to hide by being part of a large formation. Of course, there are plenty of used commercial 707s lying idle around the world which could be fitted up with fairly cheap emitters to make them appear electronically like an AWACS, but this would be a clumsy answer which would almost certainly not fool the WP staffs. Indeed, despite computer-controlled interlocking, spoof AWACS decoys might well interfere with the genuine radar of the AWACS. And all this presupposes that there will be so many hundreds of possible AWACS operating bases that the enemy missiles will fail to knock out the tiny force (at most 18 Sentries and 11 Nimrods) on the ground, which of course is far from being the case. At least the US Navy's E-2C Hawkeyes – which, though much smaller, are valuable aircraft, strictly in the AWACS class – have the advantage of a mobile airfield, which is automatically less vulnerable.

The rest of the NATO aircraft would gain in survivability by their numbers, their low altitude, their less-strident emissions, and to a small degree

from their small size, high performance and inbuilt defensive systems. It is fair to assess the overall NATO performance in the field of airborne EW as a multinational disgrace. With one or two exceptions, previously noted, the 'performance' has been non-existent, and nothing like as sophisticated as RAF Bomber or Coastal Commands' effort back in 1944. Since the mid-1970s there has been much more attention paid to this previously ignored aspect of air warfare, and the main problem is the universal one (outside the WP, it seems) of shortage of money.

Virtually all the USAF, USN and USMC tactical attack and fighter aircraft likely to operate in the European theatre have an internal passive RWR or RHAWS (radar homing and warning system), and the capability of carrying an active jammer. Not one, except for the F-111, F-14 and F-15, has an internal jammer, so carrying this important form of protection neutralises a pylon that in most cases could otherwise have been used for weapons. Far more important, the forthcoming ALQ-165 ASPJ (airborne self-protection jammer), which will be standard on most US tactical aircraft and probably on most of the remaining NATO combat aircraft, is an internal system designed to fit into a mere 2cu ft (0.065cu m), and therefore probably suitable for numerous much-needed retrofit installations. It is being produced jointly by Westinghouse and ITT.

Above:
Every tactical pilot has a healthy respect for the Soviet ZSU-23/4, the highly mobile radar-directed flak based on four 23mm guns with water-cooled barrels to permit sustained firing. Many thousands of these vehicles are in use in many countries. *Janes*

Right:
The impoverished RAF had no jamming pods after 1945 until these Westinghouse ALQ-101 (V) pods were bought secondhand from the USAF to equip Buccaneers in Germany. Though representing outdated technology, they are far better than nothing. *MoD (RAF)*

So far the only Soviet AEW aircraft positively identified is the Tu-126, called 'Moss' or SUAWACS by NATO. Based on the airframe of the Tu-114 airliner, it probably suffers from the 32 propeller blades, but there seems little justification for the derisory opinion of it held by Washington. The Indian AF found one vital in a war – entirely over land – in 1971. *UK MoD*

Modern airpower needs costly and specialised communications platforms. This Boeing E-6A of the US Navy is designed to orbit above a trailing wire aerial 26,000ft (4km) long hanging vertically from it, and similar machines are also used by the US Air Force in the EC-135 family. *Boeing*

In the meantime, active jammers of many makes are gradually being introduced to protect NATO combat aircraft. Nearly all are American, Westinghouse being the largest supplier with such mass-production families as ALQ-101, -119 and -131. The F-111 commonly carries one of these, but also has the Sanders ALQ-94 or -137 internal installation, and Sanders also makes the ALQ-126, easily the most common jammer in the US Navy and also used by KLu (Royal Netherlands AF) F-104Gs. Northrop supplies the ALQ-135 internal system of the F-15, and has several other sets in development including the ALQ-171 conformal

pallet for F-5s and the ALQ-162 and -164(V) for versions of the Harrier and AV-8C. In RAF service both the Harrier and Jaguar will eventually have internal jammers, though a decision from many proposals had not been announced by late 1984. Loral produces the ALR-56 RWR of the F-15, as well as the families of Rapport II and III integrated EW installations first used on FAB Mirage 5s and now standard on several operators of the F-16, again beginning with the FAB.

Loral is also one of the companies to have a major piece of a dedicated EW aircraft, namely the McDonnell Douglas F-4G Wild Weasel Phantom. The APR-38 system which constitutes the main onboard EW system of this aircraft has Loral displays which are served by an IBM RWR and a TI (Texas Instruments) computer. Both crew-members have a PPI (plan-position indicator) showing the rough ground position of each enemy emitter, while the backseater who operates the system has several other displays including a panoramic analysis and homing indicator. Alphanumeric displays indicate the type of threat, though at least in the early 1980s the types of WP emitter whose signatures were stored in the programme were a bit out of date. Obviously, to be of value an EW receiver system has to be programmed to recognise the hostile radars, communications and other emissions as they are, and not as they were originally – or the preceding generation! One of the advances in the

F-4G was an automatic weapon-release mode obtained by manually sighting a luminous green cursor over the threat processor's outputted red reticle in the aircraft commander's forward sight display.

The only other dedicated EW aircraft among NATO air forces is the Grumman/GD EF-111A. It is a totally rebuilt F-111A attack aircraft containing the ALR-62(V) RWR in a giant fin cap and the ALQ-99E tactical jamming system in the weapon bay. The ALQ-99E is an advanced development of the jamming system carried by the US Navy/Marines EA-6B Prowler which itself would be likely to be involved in a European war though primarily as an adjunct to Navy/Marines air strikes from carriers. The EA-6B needs a crew of four, but the EF-111A remains a two-seater thanks to improved displays, greater computer power and much better distribution of decision-taking and workload between the data processors and humans. A further big difference between the two aircraft is that in the EA-6B the actual jamming power is

packaged into external pods, each of which handles particular threat wave-bands, with emissions to front and rear, and with its own windmill-driven electric generator. The EF-111A has the entire installation mounted inside the fuselage, mostly in what was previously the weapon bay, with electric power from engine-driven generators and the jamming radiations computer-controlled and fed to aerials (antennas) inside a 19ft (5.8m) canoe fairing under the belly and in blisters on the sides of the fin. Though the whole ALQ-99E installation weighs about 6,000lb (1,814kg), at least as much as the 'black boxes' in the EA-6B, there is virtually no extra aerodynamic drag, and the EF-111A is in fact rather faster than an F-111E with a heavy external bombload. Thus it does not degrade the attack speed of a formation of NATO aircraft running in to a surface target through defended airspace, though this escort mission is just one of its roles. There are several distinct ways of using the EF-111A, for example 'barrier standoff jamming' in which the aircraft does not accompany friendly aircraft but orbits in friendly airspace, at highly variable heights and distances from the battle front line, depending on the precise demands, to provide carefully selected radiations neutralising the chief enemy air-defence threats that rely upon radar or radio emissions.

Other NATO air forces have no dedicated EW aircraft. The obvious aircraft begging to be converted for such work are the BAe Buccaneers withdrawn from Nos 15 and 16 Squadrons at Laarbruch in RAF Germany, where by the time this book appears they will have been largely replaced by Tornados. The Buccaneer has many qualities that make it ideal for use as an EW platform, notably two seats, very large internal fuel capacity for long mission endurance, speed equal to that of almost all attack aircraft including a fully loaded

swing-wing F-111 or Tornado, easy provision of adequate electric power, and an airframe which, after detailed audit, should be qualified for at least a further 10 years at low level. Like the F-4G, the Buccaneer could carry not only a comprehensive RWR and TJS (tactical jamming system) but also weapons, such as the AGM-45 Shrike and AGM-88 HARM (high-speed anti-radar missile). The EF-111A does not carry any weapons; neutralisation of the hostile threats by high explosive rather than by electronic means is left to other NATO aircraft. But if the RAF and Royal Navy have no special-purpose EW aircraft, they will soon have the world's best anti-emitter weapon in ALARM, selected in mid-1983 in preference to the older HARM. ALARM (air-launched anti-radiation missile) is smaller than the US weapon and can be carried in multiple by small fighters, for example carried like Sidewinder on the sides of major stores pylons.

Clearly the EW aspect will be central in all future major air wars, but so also will the performance of the participating aircraft and pilots. The author has already expressed his personal conviction that the obvious way to deal with hordes of invading WP aircraft is to use even greater hordes of SAMs, with plenty of reloads, and as far as possible keep all NATO aircraft out of this part of airspace. The alternative is to be forced to achieve close to perfection in a terrible IFF and recognition problem and subsequently achieve, at best, a kill ratio of roughly 2:1 in NATO's favour – which, because of the grossly dissimilar numbers of aircraft available at the outset, would mean that NATO airpower would be essentially eliminated first.

There have been countless attempts, both with dissimilar air combat research (on occasion using actual WP aircraft, such as early MiG-21s in USAF hands) and very extensive and carefully programmed computer modelling, to predict just how NATO's airpower would stack up in air combat against that of the WP nations. Most of this effort has concentrated upon the likely outcome of close combats, and not much attention has been paid to the elimination of whole airbases by missile attack, the degradation in effective fighting strength by quite sizeable armies of infiltrators (saboteurs going for key points such as surveillance radars and control centres, or death squads detailed to assassinate aircrew), the effect of chemical attack (such as used in sophisticated ways in the Far East and Afghanistan) and possibly even morale-sapping propaganda. Let us face it: nobody is going to have high morale after being suddenly jerked from a halcyon peace into the rudest of all kinds of war by a vastly more powerful enemy.

Thus cosy numerical results, such as the calculation that the F-15 would score a 913:1 victory over MiG-21s which was actually cranked out after one set of US war games, are likely to prove less than helpful. What is not in dispute is that the latest NATO air-combat aircraft, notably the F-15 and F-16, are on balance likely to win any engagement with WP aircraft on a 1 v 1 basis, and probably likely to get even better ratios on a 10 v 100 melée, though this is speculation. There is no doubt that in the first half of the 1980s these two aircraft have been superior to all others in their combination of flight performance, specific excess power, all-round agility, radar, HUD and weapons. Far more significant than hypotheses are actual combat results, and in several fairly brief but bloody engagements over Lebanon in 1982 Israeli F-15 and F-16 fighters, some of them having taken off to fly an attack mission with bombs, scored an unprecedented 84:0 victory over modern Soviet-built aircraft of the Syrian air force – or so the Israelis said.

How does one explain this dramatic result, and would it carry across to a possible conflict on the Central Sector in Europe? Whatever reasons one may adduce, the result as stated is incredible. There is always a fair measure of luck in air warfare, and Lady Luck is 100% impartial, favouring the Bad Guys (whoever they may be) along with the good. In enough engagements for 84 Syrian aircraft to be shot down there would be ample opportunity for Israeli aircraft to be lost through malfunction, pilot error, collision, IFF failure and a dozen other causes, quite apart from one being shot down by a superior opponent. The fact that the Israelis insist that they did not lose one aircraft is extraordinary.

Factors in the Israelis' favour were certainly the relative performance of the aircraft, the known excellence and aggressive professionalism of their pilots, the fact that on the whole the enemy appeared in ideal numbers – plenty of targets but never enough to present major problems – and, not least, the oustanding capability of the Israeli Grumman E-2C Hawkeye operating in the AWACS role. There is plenty of evidence to show that over modest volumes of airspace, as in the 50-mile (80km) belt east of Beirut, and in not particularly sophisticated electronic environments, the E-2C can do just about 100% of the required AWACS mission, and there would be little advantage in having a much more costly Sentry. Over Central Europe the airspace would be much larger, the number of targets perhaps 50 times greater, and the electronic environment of a different order of complexity altogether. This is not to suggest that a Hawkeye could not do a good job – far from it, and France has carefully studied the aircraft for its own Armée de l'Air – but the sheer emitted radar power, IFF capacity, data-processing capacity and speed, and other capabilities of the Sentry and Nimrod would be a possibly crucial advantage.

Given that Sentry and Nimrod can survive in European airspace, and the author must take it on trust that the NATO staffs have a positive answer to this question, there is no reason to doubt that very good results could be achieved by F-15 and F-16 aircraft in the extremely complex electronic and target environment, and worse weather, of NATO's Central Sector. But we ought not to be deluded into thinking in terms of 84:0, or anything like this. This time the opposition would be likely to have pilots not very different in capability from those of NATO, to have their own large EW capability and their own AWACS direction. The real differences would boil down to the technical superiority of the F-15 and F-16 and the probably much greater number of WP aircraft in any given block of airspace, compared with the defenders.

There is no doubt that having a significantly better air-combat fighter does exert a very large effect on the kill ratio (or, looking at it from another viewpoint, the loss ratio) in any prolonged war. Again conveniently ignoring the side issues, such as the possibility that not one F-15 or F-16 would survive a pre-emptive strike on Day 1, it would be reasonable to expect NATO air-superiority fighters to achieve a several-to-one kill ratio in any European war, but certainly not 84:0. Stand-off kills would be difficult to achieve, because at present NATO has no medium-range AAMs except Sparrow and Sky Flash which need the target to be continuously illuminated by the fighter's radar, and the large number of WP targets must mean that picking a distant enemy aircraft and flying towards it to provide radar emissions on which an AAM can home will be courting disaster from other WP aircraft at shorter ranges. The only NATO aircraft able to kill from a distance in these circumstances is the US Navy F-14, and the cost of its long-range AIM-54 Phoenix AAMs is getting on for the same as the cost of a MiG-21, so these should be preserved for really important targets.

Time and again envisaged scenarios throw up the

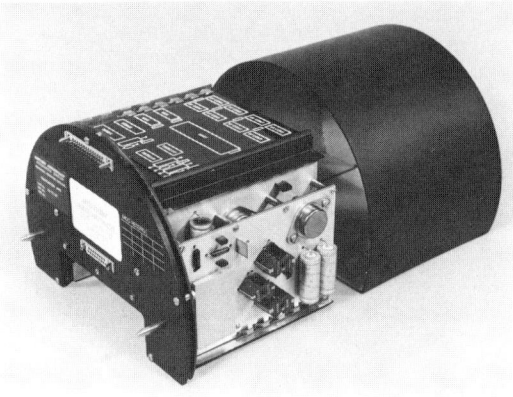

Top left:
Though the Tornado needs far less ECM support than did the F-104G, the little forward-swept HFB320 Hansa is still serving a useful role in ECM support and training. This 320 was on a quick check between missions with JaboG 32 at Lechfeld. *Rainer Karras*

Above left:
Though it seems ideal for the task, the F-16 Fighting Falcon has not yet been ordered as a Wild Weasel EW defence-suppression aircraft. This F-16B was evaluated in this role, carrying wingtip receiver pods, two HARM missiles and three Mavericks, two tanks and an ALQ-119(V) ECM pod. *GD*

Above:
Modern microelectronics make missiles smaller. This sub-miniature inertial measurement unit helps make the British Aerospace ALARM advanced anti-radar missile weigh just half the 780lb of the American HARM. Thus, RAF tactical aircraft can carry ALARM in multiple without affecting their main ordnance load. *BAe*

desperate need for AIM-120A, the advanced medium-range AAM. As noted earlier, this is a 'fire and forget' weapon, smaller than today's medium-range missiles, with autonomous mid-course inertial guidance followed by its own miniature terminal active radar to home on its target. An F-15 could carry upwards of 12 of these deadly weapons, and they would also be immediately compatible with the F-16 (which, rather surprisingly, has never been equipped to guide Sparrow), which could certainly carry eight. Later in the decade NATO's air-warfare IFF and overall C^3 electronics will be good enough for such autonomous missiles to be fired on a 'snap-shot' basis against targets up to 30 miles (48km) away, without any constraint on the NATO fighter's trajectory other than having to be briefly pointed at the target. The missile's high speed of about Mach 4 enables it to get within active-seeker homing distance of the target no matter how the latter may change direction or height. A typical flight-time would be 20sec, and even at extreme range the time would not exceed about 40sec, though it remains to be seen what a clever enemy might accomplish in that time to confuse the missile with chaff or other ECM.

One possibly important factor is that, as no CW illumination of the target is required, the enemy fighter has no prolonged warning that it is an object of interest to a NATO interceptor. Brief 'painting' by an APG-63 or -66 radar would occur so often in any future war situation that no WP aircraft would release its chaff, or go into the full ECM mode, just on this account; yet, with AMRAAM in use, that is all the indication it would get that it was being attacked – until a second or two before the kill, when it would be much too late. Certainly the NATO nations can take it for granted that a Soviet fire-and-forget AAM is in advanced development; indeed it may be one of the little-known new AAM species already assigned NATO code designations. Thus, the very great air-combat advantage gained by AMRAAM is likely to be only a temporary situation.

Incidentally, the news in late 1983 that a Sea AMRAAM is likely to be developed highlights the great value of this largely autonomous missile in the SAM role. Later in the decade it could become important as a mobile SAM for NATO ground forces, replacing Hawk as a killer of more distant targets. It would not be suitable for defence against close-range attackers, which will remain fully provided for by Rapier, and to a limited extent by Roland, Crotale and the Skyguard system.

In close-range aerial combat the factors deciding the outcome are very different from those governing the stand-off kill, and pilot quality is at least as important as aircraft performance and agility. Until 1985 the WP air forces are not expected to have any

aircraft equal in the latter parameters to the F-15 and F-16, and so far as is known the NATO fighters also continue to have better radars and displays. In the matter of weapons the contest is more equal, with the WP probably having the edge in the AA-8 'Aphid' AAM over any variant of Sidewinder. In the longer term the NATO ASRAAM will almost certainly more than keep pace with the non-stop Soviet AAM progress, but the timescale for this missile is so long that one feels anything might happen, and probably will, before a single round gets to the front-line squadrons some time in the 1990s. As for guns, US General Electric scored a major plus for the non-Communist world well over 30 years ago with its Project Vulcan development of a six-barrel rapid-fire cannon, initially in the form of the 20mm M61. Even today this gun is universal in all modern US fighters except the F-5/F-20A, and it has led to many other weapons including calibres from 5.56 to 30mm. The latter is an extremely powerful weapon primarily for use against armour, and one cannot help but feel that NATO could use considerably more than 299 external pods (as currently funded) for fitment to existing aircraft. Apart from this single gun most NATO aircraft guns have much less 'punch' per shot than the WP weapons, but the latter have lower rates of fire than the M61 and its relatives, and also normally are fed by very much smaller magazines than the M61 drums containing from 500 rounds in the F-16 to over 1,000 in the F-15 and over 2,000 when this gun is fitted to an F-111.

The only new NATO fighter gun worth mentioning is the General Electric GAU-12/U of 25mm (0.984in) calibre. In 1969-73 a different gun of this calibre was planned to launch a new generation of guns for US fighters, beginning with the F-15, but after various problems its development was abandoned and the old M61 was adopted instead. Now the new calibre has at last matured, but at present it is fitted only in the AV-8B Harrier II for the US Marine Corps. It has similar high velocity to M61, but the larger and slightly denser projectiles have a flatter trajectory, besides approximately double the destructive power. In the AV-8B ammunition has to be carried in one of the

slim belly strakes, limiting capacity to 300 rounds, but this is a useful figure that compares well with the 200 rounds of 23mm in the Soviet GP-9 pack or 100-150 rounds of 30mm per gun in the RAF Harrier or Jaguar. Ammunition capacity of either variant of Tornado is classified, but to any impartial observer it seems lunacy for NATO to use 27mm in this aircraft, two totally different kinds of 30mm in many others, 20mm in US fighters and now be introducing a 25mm!

This book happens to go to press just as the MiG-29, MiG-31 and Su-27, respectively called by NATO 'Fulcrum', 'Foxhound' and 'Flanker', are perhaps about to emerge from the shadows and become better known to the free world.

As noted earlier, the MiG-29, at first known only as 'RAM-L' after being identified in a satellite photograph of Ramenskoye test centre in early 1979, appears to be a completely new design, which is a rare thing in the Soviet Union. It has generally been policy to adopt a successful aerodynamic configuration for a range of aircraft, designed by different bureaux, ranging from small fighters to large bombers. In the matter of wings and tail the MiG-29 is perhaps a direct scale of the larger MiG-31, but Western drawings suggest that it has engine installations (believed for twin engines) similar to those of the F/A-18A Hornet, with inlets under the wing roots – where, in fact, they would be hidden from a satellite's cameras. Since about 1981 the West has been in possession of ciné film showing a MiG-29 giving a flying display, and the general consensus is that this is the most manoeuvrable air-combat fighter in the world, with thrust/weight ratio higher than that of a clean F-16. It is unquestionably intended to defeat all NATO aircraft in the air superiority role, especially at short ranges.

The MiG-31, a two-seater, could well be a scale-up of the same design, and because of its larger size it has been described as a second generation 'Foxbat' (in contrast to the MiG-25MP, 'Foxbat-E', which is simply an improved Foxbat with more powerful engines and look-down radar and shoot-down AAMs). Certainly the wings of the MiG-29 and MiG-31 appear to be the same shape,

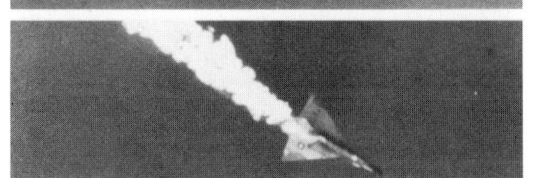

Far left:
Grumman's E-2C is a proven AEW platform, but it remains to be seen how it will stand up to the competition from the Marconi Avionics Skyguard, a modular system derived from that of the Nimrod AEW3. In theory nose and tail antennas are superior to a rotodome. *Grumman*

Left:
It is curious that the ability to fire and guide radar-guided AAMs, such as Sparrow, has never been permitted to the F-16, which in consequence has lost major export sales to the F/A-18A Hornet. Here a medium-range Sparrow is fired from a Hornet prototype. *MCAIR*

Right:
In contrast, the new AIM-120A AMRAAM (advanced medium-range AAM) does not need radar guidance from the launch aircraft, but is a valuable 'fire and forget' missile. The first AMRAAM with guidance was fired from an F-16 and destroyed a QF-102 target drone. *Hughes*

with broad chord, square tips with slim pods or missile rails, and leading edge sweep sharply increased towards the root, ending in a strake alongside the fuelage. In Chapter 2 the MiG-31 was described as 'the first true look-down shoot-down Soviet interceptor', but in fact this basic capability was the main advance incorporated in the MiG-25MP 'Foxbat-E', though the US Department of Defense (at least unitl recently) regarded this earlier interceptor as being limited in this role, and not much better than the interceptor versions of MiG-23. There is some evidence that the MiG-25MPs are rebuilds, so they presumably suffer from the same inability to manoeuvre, especially at low altitudes, that imposes such a severe limitation on the original 'Foxbat' versions of the late 1960s. It would be reasonable to assume that, in contrast, the MiG-31 has a totally different structure designed for close-combat agility at all altitudes. On the other hand, the thrust/weight ratio may not be quite as high as that of the MiG-29, because the MiG-31 probably has about four times as much internal fuel, for much greater range. It would be logical also to suppose that, while the MiG-29 is designed for front-line deployment from rough airstrips with the FA and Aviation Armies, the much heavier MiG-31 needs a long paved runway, as do all versions of the MiG-25. All this, however, is speculation.

Even less is known about the Su-27, previously called 'Ram-K' and now given the NATO reporting name of 'Flanker'. On of the few things apparently known about this aircraft is that it is a new fighter larger than the MiG-29. Thus it must be roughly the size of the MiG-31, though in the modern

inflationary world it is very unlikely that the two aircraft duplicate each other's missions and capabilities. It would be reasonable to assume, from their heritage and the meagre facts available, that the MiG-31 is a stand-off interceptor for the PVO, and the Su-27 a versatile multirole fighter in the class of the F-14, -15, -16 and -18. It is almost certainly twin-engined, and it would be reasonable to assume that it is able to operate from rough forward airstrips. Everything points to its having a variable-geometry swing-wing, and as much was suggested in several early Western reports, but in late 1983 it was impossible to confirm this. If the Su-27 has a fixed wing, there seems little point in having it as well as the MiG-31, though one difference between the two may be that the Su-27 is designed also to carry heavy attack loads and deliver these against surface targets. To the question, 'why have the Su-27 as well as the Su-24 'Fencer'?', the answer would in this case be 'because the Su-24 is a dedicated attack aircraft, with an extremely high wing-loading, and in no way could it be made into an air-superiority aircraft'.

The one continuing omission from the Soviet air armadas is a jet-lift STOVL aircraft. The Yak-36MP 'Forger' is interesting, but extremely limited, and almost irrelevant to a land war in Europe. Bearing in mind the early Soviet recognition of the need to disperse away from the known locations of airfields – and the proven value of even the first generation of operational STOVL aircraft in providing effective airpower in Operation

'Corporate', in the absence of either conventional carriers or airfields – the fact that no similar type has emerged in the WP inventory is remarkable. One conclusion may be that the WP air forces have calculated that they already have so many available locations for conventional frontal aviation airstrips that there is no need for further dispersal.

Eventually the penny must drop, if only because the demands of future air combat are independently forcing designers to move away from the crude plain jetpipe holes of the past and use vectored thrust for enhanced inflight agility. Eventually we may see the ultimate in design nonsense: a fighter with a thrust/weight ratio of about 1.3, with a vectored nozzle for use in combat, but unable to take off except from a conventional runway! Certainly the Soviets would never make such a mistake, and it would be reasonable to assume that Soviet engine testbeds are thundering with the power of several different kinds of large turbojet or turbofan with PCB (plenum-chamber burning) to vectored fan-duct nozzles and a single or twin vectored system downsteam of a rear augmenter. Full augmentation and PCB is almost a must for supersonic flight, which, even though not all that important (nothing like as important as agility, avionics and weapons), is still worth having in air superiority aircraft in order to catch the enemy or possibly to break off an engagement and escape.

It is now a decade since the US Marine Corps discovered the importance of Viffing in air combat. This technique has turned the original Harrier, which was already a very tricky air-combat opponent on account of its smokeless engine, large and very diffuse infra-red exhaust plumes, small size, odd shape and high agility, into perhaps the most frustrating aerial target at present flying. We have all read of the computer simulations and dissimilar air-combat workouts which have confirmed the unique behaviour of the Harrier and Sea Harrier as air-combat opponents, despite the fact that these aircraft have an engine designed originally in the late 1950s, and were not even intended to engage in dogfights at all! In 1987-88 RAF Germany will at last begin to get a later STOVL aircraft, the Harrier GR5 (US Harrier II), but because of lack of funds this still has essentially the same engine. Moreover, it is even more a bomber rather than a fighter, though in the period up to acceptance of the US design in July 1981 the RAF had fought for a 'big-wing Harrier' tailored to improved air combat.

What it all adds up to is that for 25 years the myopic view of the US defence establishment, and the USAF in particular, to any kind of 'not invented here' STOVL aircraft has made it very difficult to generate much enthusiasm for such machines anywhere else. Indeed, the absence of such aircraft from the Soviet inventory may be explained entirely from their absence from the USAF!

Even today we have the incredible spectacle of design teams in many NATO nations hard at work on fighter designs for the period from 1990 well into the 21st century yet still using engine thrust for horizontal propulsion only! The commonly accepted answer to the question of airfield attack continues to be 'We shall be able to take off between the craters'. Then, once in the air, some of these machines will start vectoring. Today, a decade before we get these aircraft, we already know the names and precise locations of the airfields where these fragile but costly items will be based. So do the Russians.

Below left:
The distinctive sit of the AV-8B Harrier II will progressively become familiar in Western military circles. *MCAIR*

Below:
The Harrier GR5, which differs from the AV-8B in radar-warning system, gun and many other details, besides having two extra wing stores pylons, is likely to be deployed inititally, and perhaps solely, in RAF Germany – it is to be hoped that they do not spend their non-flying time parked at pre-targeted locations. Pilots will find their flight workload reduced, especially during take-off and landing. *McDonnell Douglas*

Glossary

AAA	anti-aircraft artillery
AAM	air-to-air missile
AASU	Aviation Armies of the Soviet Union
ABM	anti-ballistic missile
ADOC	Air-Defence Operations Centre
ADSM	air-defence suppression missile
ADV	air defence variant
AEW	airborne early warning
AFV	armoured fighting vehicle
AI	air intercept
ALARM	Air-Launched Anti-Radar Missile
ALCM	Air-Launched Cruise Missile
AMI	Italian air force
AMRAAM	Advanced Medium-Range Air-to-Air Missile
AP	armour piercing
ASM	air-to-surface missile
ASRAAM	Advanced Short-Range Air-to-Air Missile
ASW	Anti-submarine warfare
AVMF	air forces of the Soviet navy
AWACS	Airborne Warning And Control System
BVR	beyond visual range
C^2	command and control
C^3	command, control and communications
CAP	combat air patrol
CBW	chemical/biological warfare
CCV	control-configured vehicle
CPSU	Communist Party of the Soviet Union
CW	continuous-wave radiation
DA	Soviet long-range aviation
DACT	dissimilar air-combat training
DME	distance-measuring equipment
ECM	electronic countermeasures
Elint	electronic intelligence
ESM	electronic support (or surveillance) measures
EW	electronic warfare
FA	*Frontovoya Aviatsiya*, or Soviet frontal aviation (tactical air force)
FAB	Belgian air force
FLIR	forward looking infra-red
FOL	forward operating location
GKO	Soviet State Defence Committee
GSFG	Group of Soviet Forces in Germany
HARM	High-speed Anti-Radar Missile
HAS	hardened aircraft shelter

HE	high-explosive
HUD	head-up display
ICBM	intercontinental ballistic missile
IDS	interdictor strike
IFF	identification friend or foe
IIR	imaging infra-red
INF	intermediate-range nuclear force(s)
INS	inertial navigation system
IR	infra-red
JTIDS	Joint Tactical Information Distribution System
KLu	Netherlands air force
KNL	Norwegian air force
LANTIRN	low-altitude navigational tageting IR for night
LGB	laser-guided bomb
MIRV	multiple individually-targeted re-entry vehicle(s)
MTI	moving-target indication
NATO	North Atlantic Treaty Organisation
NADGE	NATO Air Defence Ground Environment
NBC	nuclear, biological, chemical
NICS	NATO Integrated Communications System
OMG	Operational Manoevre Group (Soviet)
PRF	pulse-repetition frequency
PVO	Soviet aerospace defence of the homeland
RDF	Rapid Deployment Force (US)
RGWS	radar-guided weapons system
RVSN	Soviet strategic rocket forces
RWR	radar warning receiver
SACEUR	Supreme Allied Commander Europe
SAM	surface-to-air missile
SAR	search and rescue/synthetic-aperture radar
SEP	specific excess power
SIF	selective identification facility
SLBM	submarine-launched ballistic missile
SSBS	French strategic nuclear missiles
STOVL	Short takeoff, vertical landing
Tacan	tactical air navigation
TARPS	Tactical Air Reconnaissance Pod System
TFS	Tactical Fighter Squadron
TFTW	Tactical Fighter Training Wing
TFW	Tactical Fighter Wing
TNF	theatre nuclear force(s)
TRW	Tactical Reconnaissance Wing
Triple-A	AAA; anti-aircraft artillery
TVD	theatre of military/war operation (Soviet)
TVM	track via missile (SAM guidance)
T/W	thrust-to-weight
UKADGE	United Kingdom Air Defence Ground Environment
USAF(E)	United States Air Force (Europe)
USMC	US Marine Corps
USN	US Navy
VGK	Soviet supreme high command
VOR	VHF omnirange
VTA	Soviet war transport aviation
VVS	*Voyenno Vozdushnye Sili*, or Soviet air force
WP	Warsaw Pact